Help for Questioning Christians

Help for Questioning Christians

*What Contemporary Scholars
Are Saying About "Settled" Moral Issues*

JOHN T. WHITEHEAD

RESOURCE *Publications* • Eugene, Oregon

HELP FOR QUESTIONING CHRISTIANS
What Contemporary Scholars Are Saying About "Settled" Moral Issues

Copyright © 2025 John T. Whitehead. All rights reserved. Except for brief quotations in critical publications or reviews, no part of this book may be reproduced in any manner without prior written permission from the publisher. Write: Permissions, Wipf and Stock Publishers, 199 W. 8th Ave., Suite 3, Eugene, OR 97401.

Resource Publications
An Imprint of Wipf and Stock Publishers
199 W. 8th Ave., Suite 3
Eugene, OR 97401

www.wipfandstock.com

PAPERBACK ISBN: 979-8-3852-3183-6
HARDCOVER ISBN: 979-8-3852-3184-3
EBOOK ISBN: 979-8-3852-3185-0

Dedicated to

Pat, my love, and best friend,

Dan, Tim, and Fluffy,

And

Seekers of the truth

Contents

Preface xi
Abbreviations xii

Chapter 1: Introduction: Settled and Not So Settled Issues 1
    Introduction 1
    What the Polls Say 3
    Objective 4
    A Note on Progressive Christianity 8
    Conclusion 9

Chapter 2: The Prosperity Gospel: From Abundance to Blaming the Poor 11
    The Prosperity Gospel: Version I 12
    The Prosperity Gospel: Version II 13
    Comparison with the Message of Jesus 17
    God Does Not Always Deliver What You Asked For 18
    Coda: Prosperity Gospel Redux: Let the Poor Eat Cake But Only If They Earn the Money to Buy Their Own Cake 20
    Conclusion 22

Chapter 3: Afterlife: Heaven and Hell: What Happens After We Die? 23
    Introduction 23
    The Teaching of the Churches 24
    Polling on Belief in Hell 26
    Historian Bart Ehrman 26
    Alcorn: A Traditional View of Hell Plus 27

CONTENTS

 Rabbi Blech: A Softer, Gentler Version of Hell 28
 Hell for a Philosopher: Joshua Rasmussen 28
 A Progressive Christianity Discussion of Hell 29
 Conclusion on Hell 30
 Heaven 30
 The Teaching of the Churches 31
 What Will Make You Happy? 32
 Rabbi Blech on Heaven 32
 Alcorn's View of Heaven 33
 N. T. Wright: Less Emphasis on Heaven 34
 Miller's Comments 35
 Is a Perfect World (Heaven) Boring? 36
 Sidebar: Who Goes to Heaven? 37
 Conclusion 37

Chapter 4: Pre-Marital Sex: From Graduate School to Old Age 39
 Introduction 39
 Poll Data 40
 Two Theologians on Sexuality 41
  Knust's Reliance on Scripture 41
  The View of Peters 42
 Two Contemporary Situations 44
 Moultrie: Erotic Justice 46
 Ellison: A Progressive Christianity View 46
 Married Persons with a Spouse with Alzheimer's Disease:
  A Special Case of Extra-Marital Sex 47
 Comparison 48
 Conclusion 49

Chapter 5: Homosexual Intimacy: Embracing Celibacy
  vs. Seeking Connection 51
 Introduction 51
 Public Opinion 54
 Theologians 54
 Traditional View of Homosexuality vs. Traditional View of Marriage 57
 Psychology 57
 Gay Voices 58

Contents

Comparison 60
Conclusion 61

Chapter 6: Divorce 64
Introduction 64
Divorce in the New Testament 65
The Teaching of the Churches 65
The Catholic Church and the Issue of Annulments 67
Ellison's Progressive Christianity View 69
A "Pastoral" Approach 70
Conclusion: Compassionate View of Divorce versus Strict Positions on Other Issues 71

Chapter 7: Abortion: Two Meanings of Respect for Life, the Right to Choose, and the Lesson of the Good Samaritan Parable 73
Introduction 73
Historical Notes 74
What the Churches Say 75
Poll Results 77
Dworkin 78
McGlasson on Abortion 80
Collins and the Question of Biblical Values 81
Peters on Abortion: 82
Kamitsuka 84
Ellison 86
Gutman and Moreno 88
Comparison 88
Adoption: A False Alternative 89
Conclusion 91

Chapter 8: Physician-Assisted Suicide 94
Introduction 94
Hardwig: A Duty to Die 96
The Catholic Position 98
Collins on the Bible and Euthanasia 99
The Suicide Tourist 100
The Pro-Life Response to *The Suicide Tourist* 101
The Dutch Experience 101

Contents

    Dworkin's Argument 102
    Another Dworkin's View 104
    The Human/Humane Argument 104
    Comparison 106
    Conclusion 108

Chapter 9: The Death Penalty 110
    Introduction 110
    The Teaching of Several Churches 111
    Criminologists 112
    Theologians on the Death Penalty 114
    Life Sentences 119
    Conclusion 123

Chapter 10: Religion and Politics: From Presidential Elections to Christian Nationalism to "Let Them Eat Cake" 125
    Introduction 125
    Christians and Elections 126
    History 128
    Christianity and Culture: White Christian Nationalism 130
    Wedding Cakes, Websites, and Gay Marriage 135
    Implications of Catholic Church Blessings of Same-Sex Couples on the Issue of Baking a Wedding Cake or Creating a Website for a Gay Couple 136
    Religion and Healthcare 137
    Extent of Religious Influence 138
    Common Features 138
    Conclusion 139

Chapter 11: Conclusion: Where Do We Go from Here? 142
    Introduction 142
    Recent Developments 143
    Where We Are: Summary of Analyses 145
    Where We Are Going: Implications 147
    Difficulty of Accepting New Views 151
    Conclusion 154

Bibliography 157

Preface

I WANT TO THANK Michael Braswell for his helpful suggestions about the subject matter throughout the time I worked on this book and for his critical suggestions in seeking a publisher. Mickey has always been a close friend and someone I can talk with about the important matters in life. Without his help, this book would not have been written.

I also want to thank Colin Baxter for his encouragement and for writing a comment piece that appears on the back cover.

Finally, the book is meant to be a conversation starter, not a conversation stopper. The topics discussed are serious and need thorough study, reflection, and prayer. Hopefully, the discussion in this book can help believers in their own struggles to discern what is ethical as they try to live a meaningful and ethical life.

Abbreviations

Catechism of the Catholic Church (CCC)
Evangelical Lutheran Church in America (ELCA)
Southern Baptist Convention (SBC)
United States Conference of Catholic Bishops (USCCB)

CHAPTER 1

Introduction: Settled and Not So Settled Issues

Examples of Violations: "sexual relations outside a biblically ordained marriage; romantic displays of affection with a member of the same sex (e.g., hand-holding, kissing, dating, etc.)."—Liberty University Honor Code 2024–2025

"While God loves the homosexual and offers salvation, homosexuality is not a normal lifestyle and is an abomination in the eyes of God."
—Southern Baptist Convention

"The God that holds you over the pit of hell, much as one holds a spider . . . abhors you, and is dreadfully provoked: his wrath towards you burns like fire; he looks upon you as worthy of nothing else, but to be cast into the fire."
—Jonathan Edwards

INTRODUCTION

MANY CHRISTIANS MAY THINK that every moral issue is settled. Abortion and pre-marital sex are wrong; gay marriage is not possible; physician-assisted suicide is sinful; an eternal hell awaits the sinner who does not repent. Preachers, televangelists, and official church teaching convey the message that moral issues are clear-cut. Often a church goes so far as to cut off debate. The Catholic Church offers no room for questioning of its teaching that abortion is wrong and has recently called gender-affirming surgery and surrogacy grave violations of human dignity.[1] A Catholic who appears to support freedom of choice risks being denied communion by the local bishop, as evidenced by calls to deny the sacrament to President Biden. The Southern Baptist Convention (SBC) drops individual churches that do not follow church teaching on homosexuality or women. In fact, the SBC recently reaffirmed its removal of Rick Warren's Saddleback Church because that church veers from SBC's statement of faith which holds that the office of pastor is limited to men.[2] One SBC authority stated that the SBC will automatically endorse a Republican candidate for president because there is no room for debate on abortion.[3] The Methodist Church recently split over the issue of LGBTQIA+ rights. Similarly, Lee University had proposed a policy that would ban faculty or students from even discussing nontraditional sexual behaviors or lifestyles in a positive fashion:

> No member of the Lee University community may promote or advocate, in person, in writing, or online, for sexual acts, behaviors or lifestyles that are contrary to Scripture, this statement of belief, or any other university policy.[4]

This proposed statement was later changed to:

> We commit to engaging in discussion of topics such as sexuality, same-sex sexual behavior, same-sex attraction, sexual orientation, sexual identity, and gender identity with grace and humility, always directing each other toward God's grace and truth in this fallen world.[5]

While many Christians and Christian churches consider such moral issues beyond debate, theologians and other scholars have presented different positions. Some theologians dispute the interpretation of the Bible that underlies the settled answer. Others note that changed circumstances call for fresh approaches; that Jesus did not even confront a particular issue when He practiced His ministry some two thousand years ago. Still others

---

1. Dicastery for the Doctrine of the Faith, *Infinite Dignity*.
2. Andone and Nottingham, "Southern Baptist Convention Votes."
3. Smith, "Southern Baptists Considering."
4. News Channel 9, "Some Students."
5. Lee University, "Statement of Beliefs."

INTRODUCTION: SETTLED AND NOT SO SETTLED ISSUES

go beyond the Bible to present reasoned arguments for fresh approaches. Philosophers also rely on rational arguments. Psychologists and criminologists rely on both empirical data and logical reasoning to address ethical issues.

For the average Christian struggling to decide what is ethical, there may be little or no awareness that what one hears in church, watches on television, or reads in church documents does not necessarily match what contemporary scholars are saying about critical moral issues. Professors of theology, Scripture, history, law, and the social sciences have presented claims that go contrary to what many believers think is settled doctrine.

WHAT THE POLLS SAY

Although the average Christian may be unaware that there are theologians who present positions contrary to official church teaching, that average Christian may listen to or read an orthodox message but practice contrary behavior. Substantial percentages of churchgoers are ignoring or disagree with what their preacher preaches on Sunday and even what their church teaches in official pronouncements. While Catholic and Southern Baptist preachers and church resolutions say that homosexuality, abortion, and premarital sex are sinful, many Americans disagree with or disregard traditional teaching. Seventy-one percent of all Americans and 40 percent of weekly churchgoers support same-sex marriage being legal.[6] A majority of Americans and many church members say that abortion should be legal in all or most cases and that *Roe v. Wade* should not have been overturned. Specifically, 62 percent of all Americans, 61 percent of white non-evangelical Protestants, 71 percent of black Protestants and 60 percent of Catholics support abortion being legal in all or most cases. On the other hand, 73 percent of white evangelical Protestants think that abortion should be illegal in all or most cases. And 83 percent of religiously unaffiliated Americans think it should be legal in all or most cases.[7] Also contrary to much church teaching, in an October 2019 survey, the Pew Research Center found that 45 percent of mainline Protestants and 40 percent of Catholics stated that sex between unmarried adults in a committed relationship is always

---

6. McCarthy, "Same-Sex Marriage Support."
7. Blazina, "Key Facts."

acceptable. In that same survey, 50 percent of Christians stated that *casual sex is always or sometimes acceptable*.[8]

The customary response to such numbers is pollster George Barna's claim that Christians who support "immoral" actions are not *authentic* Christians or that they are misguided or simply sinners.[9] This line of thinking has even caused denominations to split apart, such as the recent split in the Methodist Church. What this book will show is that there are both theologians and other scholars who present significant arguments contrary to traditional positions. So, although the intent of this book is not to provide churchgoers with excuses for engaging in behaviors contrary to the teaching of their church body, we will examine theological positions that do contradict several church teachings and could be used to justify actions contrary to church beliefs.

OBJECTIVE

The aim of this book is to help Christians struggling to do the right thing by exploring the views that some theologians, philosophers, and social scientists present about critical moral issues that many Christians and churches consider settled. Specifically, while major religious bodies have presented clearcut teaching on abortion, premarital sex, divorce, euthanasia, the death penalty, hell, and the Prosperity Gospel, in each of these areas there are scholars who present an alternative position. So if one's pastor or priest is preaching the official teaching of that church, there are theologians who offer a different perspective. Additionally, on a number of these topics there are other churches that take a position contrary to what many think is the traditional and certainly correct position.

In 2023 there was some indication that the Catholic Church might be open to change on some issues that it has traditionally considered closed. In late 2023 Pope Francis ruled that priests may offer a blessing on same-sex married couples.[10] In October 2023 the Synod on Synodality noted that certain issues, such as "matters of identity and sexuality, the end of life, complicated marital situations, and ethical issues related to artificial intelligence," "raise new questions" and need "reflection" and

---

8. Diamant, "Christians Say."
9. Salai, "Barna Study Suggests."
10. Sullivan, "Pope Francis Approves."

"further clarification."[11] On April 2, 2024, however, the Doctrine Office of the Vatican released the Declaration "Infinite Dignity" which rejected gender theory and sex change interventions, and reiterated the Church's opposition to abortion and euthanasia.[12] This document, therefore, suggests that Pope Francis is still very traditional on critical moral issues.

Conservative Christians, including Catholics, Southern Baptists, Missouri Synod Lutherans, and others, may be thinking that their church teaches the correct answer and they have no need for a book like this. At the very least, however, the discussion may help them understand why other Christians and non-Christians take a non-traditional approach. Second, personal dilemmas pertaining to each ethical issue may resonate independently of scholarly debates. Although one's church says abortion, homosexual sexual activity, and physician-assisted suicide are sinful, when a believer or a believer's child faces one of these issues, the traditional answer may not seem so simple. So Christians may have dismissed traditional answers after facing a direct decision about abortion, homosexual actions, or euthanasia and this book can help them find intellectual justifications for their earlier personal decisions. Christians who have stopped going to church (see discussion of the "nones" below) may have done so due to discomfort with traditional ethical teachings. The fact that theologians offer non-traditional ethical arguments may help them feel that they can still be a Christian even if they do not follow conservative teaching. All parties can benefit by showing all that there are analyses out there that they may never have considered themselves.

One reason such an exploration is necessary is the ongoing decline in church membership and attendance. The Pew Research Center reports an ongoing decrease of Americans since the 1990s who say they are Christian versus a continual increase of those leaving traditional Christianity to call themselves atheists, agnostics, or "nothing in particular." While about 64 percent of Americans currently self-identify as Christian, that percentage could drop to 54 percent or even 35 percent by 2070 and the percentage of "nones" (atheists, agnostics, and "nothing in particular" combined) could rise from 28 percent to between one-third to over half of the U.S. population.[13] Similarly, Silliman (2021) notes a precipitous drop in the evangelical

---

11. U.S. Conference of Catholic Bishops, *A Synodal Church*.
12. Dicastery for the Doctrine of the Faith, *Infinite Dignity*.
13. Jones, "Church Attendance."

book market and the disappearance of the Christian bookstore.[14] Gibson states that the Catholic Church in the U.S. is in "exodus and crisis" as the Church is facing a reality of fewer priests, fewer deacons, fewer lay ministers, and declining church attendance. So today Catholics make up one-fifth or less of the U.S. population, versus one quarter a generation ago.[15] Davis, Graham, and Burge describe the loss of forty million church members as "the largest and fastest religious shift in the history of our country."[16] One reason for this ongoing exodus and drop in church attendance might be dissatisfaction with traditional moral positions. As noted, many Americans approve of abortion, physician-assisted suicide, and premarital sexual intercourse. If church leaders want to address the growing numbers of Christians who are switching from identifying as "Christian" to "none" and stop the decline in attendance, they should be aware of the dissatisfaction. Only then, can they address it. This does not mean that churches simply abandon traditional teaching. It suggests that church leaders be prepared to discuss and debate the concerns of their congregants.

Another reason for this examination is to prevent further denominational splits. If both conservative and liberal members of a denomination have a deeper understanding of the issues they disagree on, then perhaps they can learn to accept the position that the settled answer is not the only approach. Perhaps they can come to see why some church members disagree with the traditional answer and not simply call for the members on each side to split into two separate churches.

The broader goal is to help all Christians—those who accept the settled answers, those who disagree, and the undecided—make better informed ethical decisions. It is assumed that most Christians are familiar with traditional Church teaching. Many churchgoers, however, may not be aware that scholars have presented points of view that differ from traditional teaching. While official church positions declare that abortion is wrong, some scholars argue that the Bible takes no position on abortion. While conservative churches reaffirm belief in a traditional hell, one scholar argues that Jesus did not say that sinners go to hell and another maintains that the maximum time in hell is twelve months, not eternity! While some Christians argue that Jesus' parable of the Good Samaritan teaches that every pregnant woman should care for the fetus as the Good

---

14. Silliman, *Reading Evangelicals*.
15. Gibson, "What Happens Now?," 31–35.
16. Davis et al., *The Great Dechurching*, 3.

INTRODUCTION: SETTLED AND NOT SO SETTLED ISSUES

Samaritan cared for the victim of a roadside bandit, one scholar shows the illogical reasoning of that argument. While the SBC teaches that Paul's Letter to the Romans endorses capital punishment, the current consensus of criminologists is that the death penalty has no proven impact on deterrence, is fraught with mistakes, is terribly expensive, and cannot determine who the worst murderers are who would theoretically deserve the death penalty. While several churches condemn premarital sex, several religious scholars see no contradiction between the Bible and some premarital relationships. There is even a suggestion that a senior citizen Christian with a spouse suffering from Alzheimer's disease is permitted to engage in a sexual relationship because his spouse has "abandoned" him/her! While several churches condemn physician-assisted suicide, one philosopher sees it as ethical and goes so far as to say that in certain cases there may be an ethical duty to die! Another philosopher argues that life is not just physical subsistence but also each individual's attempt to live a meaningful life. When a meaningful life is no longer possible, suicide is an option because it shows respect for an individual's desire to live a meaningful life. While many Christians believe that the United States is a Christian nation, writers such as Andrew Whitehead dispute that claim and explain the dangerous implications of that belief.[17]

So the objective of this book is to inform readers about nontraditional positions on several ethical issues. On each ethical issue, we will offer scholarly positions that differ from traditional positions. The intent is not to convince believers that the traditional position is wrong, but to show what some scholars are saying. Our position is that when making an ethical decision, the best approach is to be aware of as much information and reasoning as possible. Similarly, if a traditionalist wishes to convince others of the truth of the traditional position, he or she needs to be aware of nontraditional positions. If one has no awareness of what the other thinks or believes, she will not be ready to understand and discuss what the ethical course of action is concerning the topics covered in this book. A traditionalist will not have any impact on a questioner if the traditionalist has no understanding of the questioner's concerns.

In the political sphere a major problem is that both the right and the left have given up trying to even listen to the other side. People on the right listen to talk radio and watch outlets such as Fox News. People on the left listen to their talk radio stations and watch outlets such as MSNBC. The

---

17. Whitehead, *American Idolatry*.

refusal to even consider the other point of view is the basis for many of the political problems facing America today. Instead of honest debate and compromise, we have partisan single-mindedness and a refusal to try to come up with answers for many of the problems facing the country. Just as citizens need to listen to both sides of the political spectrum, churchgoers need to be aware of debates and developments in theology, philosophy, and the social sciences that involve critical ethical issues.

A caveat: Although the chapters will discuss some of the arguments and reasoning in favor of the traditional answers, the main focus is on writers who present alternative approaches. So readers looking for a deeper understanding of traditional answers need to look for current writers who are perhaps offering newer takes on the traditional direction or are trying to refute the type of argumentation that is the focus of this book. It is assumed that readers are familiar with traditional approaches, but readers are encouraged to seek out religious writers who embrace such approaches in order to make a fully informed and fully thought-out decision about any of the issues discussed in this book. Furthermore, there is no intention to endorse an "anything goes" ethic. The issues of premarital sex, abortion, which candidate to vote for, and physician-assisted suicide are serious issues and believers need to be informed and to think and pray about their decisions. Hopefully, this book can offer some information but that is only part of the decision process.

A NOTE ON PROGRESSIVE CHRISTIANITY

Young claims that most Protestant denominations have split into a liberal or progressive church and an evangelical or conservative church. He also contends that Progressive Christianity is fundamentally flawed as it has embraced contemporary secular points of view and turned its back on authentic Christian beliefs, even to the point of rejecting belief in the divinity of Christ.[18]

In this book we chose not to approach all the ethical issues discussed from a simple Progressive Christianity vs. Conservative Christianity label. First, we wanted to avoid simplifying all these issues into a simple Progressive or Liberal vs. Conservative debate. For example, the debate on capital punishment between Catholics and Southern Baptists is a debate between two conservative denominations. Similarly, the question of the Prosperity

18. Young, *A Grand Illusion*.

Gospel is not a Progressive/Conservative one. Second, on all of the issues we presented what scholars had to say about what the Bible says on the issue, if anything, whereas Young contends that Progressive Christians give insufficient weight to what the Bible has to say. For example, we outlined the biblical differences between the Catholic Church and the SBC on capital punishment. On divorce we noted the crucial debate over what the Gospels say. Third, it seems that historical and scientific developments have more to say about issues such as homosexuality, gay marriage, and premarital sex than about core doctrines such as the divinity of Christ.

This book does discuss the positions of some Progressive Christianity writers, such as Peters in the abortion chapter. Such writers are included because their ideas seem worth considering, regardless of where they stand on more fundamental issues such as the divinity of Christ. We leave a thorough discussion of Progressive Christianity or liberal theology to other writers.

CONCLUSION

Each chapter will analyze positions of theologians or other scholars who offer an alternative to traditional teaching on critical moral issues. The concluding chapter will attempt to pull together some common insights from the specific analyses of each topic. In several instances there does appear to be enough evidence or reasoning for some clear resolution. The main objective, however, is to offer alternative perspectives and let each reader decide which viewpoint, traditional or alternative, seems the better alternative.

There is no claim that this is a comprehensive discussion of all the ethical issues chosen. The aim is to introduce readers—believers ranging from devout churchgoers to Christians in name only and also non-believers concerned about ethical issues—to points of view that they were not aware exist. By presenting viewpoints that differ from traditional Christian teaching, we hope to broaden the perspective of all Christians. If so, perhaps progress can be made in reconciling traditional and nontraditional approaches to abortion, homosexuality, gay marriage, and physician-assisted suicide. Rather than immediately asserting that all of these things are unethical and even sinful, it is hoped that presenting what a number of scholars have to say on these topics can broaden the discussion. For one, misconceptions may exist. One may think that Jesus actually said that X is wrong when in fact He said little or nothing about that issue. Second, in some cases, the issue was not really an issue in the time of Jesus. For example, physician-assisted suicide was not a problem at about 30 C.E. Life expectancy was much shorter and the state of medicine was much less advanced. It is the hope that readers on all sides of these issues can benefit from looking at contemporary scholarship. It is not anticipated that differences will somehow suddenly disappear. It is simply hoped that debate and discussion can help all readers, traditional or nontraditional, have a clearer understanding of each ethical issue so that whatever stance one takes, that stance is a fully informed and fully considered decision. It is also hoped that this book may help prevent further denominational splits. If both sides on an issue have a clearer understanding of the other side, perhaps that will enable the two sides to continue to worship together rather than go through an acrimonious split.

It needs to be noted that there is the utmost respect for the churches and the believers that teach and adhere to traditional positions. It is understood that both churches and individuals are sincerely seeking to discern what God wants them to do and to uphold as the ethical course of action. This book simply notes that there are sincere writers out there who do question traditional teaching.

For those Christians who question traditional answers, this book can alert them to scholarly positions that they have not read. By reading about those scholars and also trying to learn more about traditional theologians, questioning Christians can be better informed to choose the ethical course of action that study, prayer, and reflection suggest is the best course of action. It might even turn out that reading about contemporary scholars may influence questioning Christians to re-embrace traditional positions.

CHAPTER 2

The Prosperity Gospel: From Abundance to Blaming the Poor

"I tried poverty and I didn't like it."—Oral Roberts

"And he said to them, 'Take care! Be on your guard against all kinds of greed; for one's life does not consist in the abundance of possessions.'"—Luke 12:15

"Get ready for favor that you haven't seen, for opportunity, influence, and promotion. He has something out of the ordinary, something impressive, a new level coming your way."—Joel Osteen

AN INTRIGUING STARTING POINT is the so-called Prosperity Gospel. Millions of television viewers watch celebrity status televangelists preach this Gospel on Sunday. Many Christians belong to megachurches which are the temples of this Gospel. Almost 40 percent of Protestants subscribe to the Prosperity Gospel.[1]

Actually, there are two versions of the Prosperity Gospel: one might be labeled the "Righteous Gemstones" version while there is a more subtle version that has some truth to it. Both promise prosperity or abundance: God wants to make all of His children prosper. So He rewards faith and prayer with abundance.

---

1. *Relevant*, "Report."

THE PROSPERITY GOSPEL: VERSION I

An example of the first or questionable version is prosperity preacher Mike Murdock. Murdock, actually "Doctor" Murdock, likes to tell how he made a donation to his church and God quickly responded. The donation was not that sizable because he did not have that much money, but it was about all he had at the time. Because he gave even when it hurt, God quickly inspired some women in the church to take him to a custom tailor and order four custom made suits for him!

On a show aired on June 14, 2015 on a station in my area, Murdock stated that he had a sudden vision about a man who had just lost his job. Despite this job loss, Murdock advised this man to send in a seed of fifty-eight dollars. Murdock told the man to use his credit card, sow the "seed" of fifty-eight dollars and then he would receive "the best job he's ever had in his lifetime."

As Dr. Murdock was promising this man "the best job he's ever had in his lifetime," the show was flashing this warning on the screen: "Miracles are a blessing of God. Inspiration Ministries does not guarantee miracles for everyone who gives." So the official "ministry" of Murdock was posting a disclaimer at the exact same time that its star minister was doing what the warning advised against, namely, promising a miracle.

Later, Murdock upped the ante. He asserted that God wants 300 people to send in a thousand dollars each. God will answer this faith commitment by making each a millionaire! As an aside, one of his arguments for sending in the sum of $1,000 was that you can't do much with just a thousand dollars anyway, so why not trade it in for a million![2]

Older examples of the first version of Prosperity Theology are Robert Tilton and a televangelist I will label Evangelist P. Investigations showed that Tilton hired workers to remove checks and cash out of envelopes and throw away the prayer requests he had encouraged viewers to send him.[3] The writer watched one of P.'s television shows as he claimed that God had cured diabetes for some of his audience members, a claim that contradicts normal medical practice.

A reincarnation of P. and his promises of miracle cures is Bishop Joshua. Airing on the Living Faith Network, Bishop Joshua's television show

---

2. For more on Murdock, see Lieber, "This Prosperity Preacher."
3. Branstetter, "Robert Tilton."

proudly proclaims, "By faith you can overcome any health problem."[4] On one show Joshua claimed he healed one woman from blindness and another woman from back pain for which a doctor had recommended surgery. To a caller suffering from diabetes, high blood pressure, and prostate cancer, the Bishop promised healing "very soon."[5] Note: Bishop Joshua cannot prove his claims and it would be difficult to disprove them with absolute certainty.

Mainstream Christian denominations do not promise followers certain millionaire status or miracle cures if they have faith or just send in their "vows"—Murdock had confiscated the religious term "vow" to cover a donation to him—as soon as possible. Mainstream denominations do allow for possible miracle cures and for people perhaps getting monetary windfalls. But that is not the heart of their message.

THE PROSPERITY GOSPEL: VERSION II

Joel Osteen is the more subtle face of the Prosperity Gospel. Bowler labels his message *soft* prosperity instead of the *hard* prosperity message of Murdock and his ilk.[6] Osteen appears on television regularly on various networks and local stations and even has his own App. He is photogenic and has a very upbeat message. If you watch or listen to him on any venue, you get a believable and positive message. Basically, that message is that God will bestow abundant blessings on you if you believe, pray, and hope. For example, Osteen states that "God didn't make you to be average; God created you to excel."[7] And God doesn't want his children to ask simply for small favors such as a minimal raise: "Think big. Think increase. Think abundance. Think more than enough."[8] Joel advises his followers to ask God for fame: "…pray, 'God make me famous in my field. Let me shine. Give me influence.'"[9]

Osteen writes a new book about every year and is on television and Sirius XM radio. His books and sermons continue to offer fresh variations of the core Prosperity Gospel message.

---

4. Show aired Sept. 11, 2020.
5. Show aired Sept. 11, 2020.
6. Bowler, *Blessed*.
7. Osteen, *Become a Better You*, 82.
8. Osteen, *Become a Better You*, 11. See also Osteen, *Blessed in the Darkness*.
9. Osteen, *Think Better*, 145.

So God bestows blessings, but not just "spiritual blessings." God is just waiting to give believers a great job, a beautiful home, and lots of money. His message is quite popular. One writer describes Osteen as "America's most powerful twenty-first century evangelical minister."[10]

One of Osteen's prime examples of belief in prosperity or abundance thinking is how he came to get the Compaq Center for his church in Houston. Joel was looking for a new building for his services. Twice he thought he had a deal for a building but both times the deal fell through. Then the Compaq Center, a venue much better than the two venue deals that fell through, became available and this shows that God has abundance in store for you if you just have patience and faith.[11] If your girlfriend or boyfriend dumps you, fear not. God has a better mate for you down the road. If you are in a low paying job, fear not. God has a high paying job for you just around the corner. If your lawyer tells you that the city is not going to sell you the Compaq Center, get a different lawyer.[12]

Osteen also claims that God "supernaturally healed" his mother from cancer in 1981. When she was diagnosed, she kept reciting Scripture passages until she was healed. He tells readers that "You can do the same thing."[13] Or as one of his recent books says, "If the medical report doesn't look good, while you're taking the treatment you have to say, Father, thank you that greater health is coming."[14]

Although Joel himself has not been the direct benefactor of a healing from God, he has benefited physically in what Sinitiere calls Osteen's "prosperity gospel of the body," namely, that faith in God leads not only to financial prosperity but also to "good health, emotional wholeness, and psychological well-being."[15] In other words, Joel preaches a gospel "not just of faith and finances, but also of faith and fitness."[16] Evidence for this aspect of Osteen's message is that in 2012 Osteen must have prayed a lot, or visited the gym quite frequently, because a website and a magazine article with

---

10. Sinitiere, "Salvation with a Smile."
11. Osteen, *Think Better*.
12. Osteen, *Your Greater*.
13. Osteen Website.
14. Osteen, *Rule Your Day*, 3.
15. Sinitiere, "Salvation with a Smile," 90.
16. Sinitiere, "Salvation with a Smile," 89.

photos described him as "ripped" with a sculpted body. Later, he was acclaimed to be number one on the list of Top 10 Fittest Christian Leaders.[17]

So the message of the Prosperity preachers is simple: Believe and Pray and Donate to these preachers and God will reward you with abundance, including financial prosperity or a cure for your cancer or a great set of abs! Thus, in the megachurches, tithing becomes the peak of the service. In turn, the financial success of the leaders, shown by expensive cars and private jets, makes them "tangible reminders of God's goodness and the abundant provisions in store for all who believed."[18]

Many Prosperity Gospel believers link belief in God with health. For example, almost two-thirds of American Pentecostals say that they themselves have been healed or they know someone who has been healed. Many go so far as to believe they do not need medicine or doctors; they see seeking medical assistance as evidence of lack of faith in God.[19]

It seems that most of the time when Osteen seems to be espousing the Prosperity Gospel he just focuses on the positive things that God will give the faithful believer: health, wealth, a new boyfriend or girlfriend. To be fair to Osteen, however, in his 2016 book he writes that part of the reason for asking God for favor is to benefit others. For example, he tells doctors to ask God for fame and influence, to ask God for the chance to develop new "procedures that benefit mankind. Then use that influence to help those who can't afford it."[20] This reason for asking for God's favor does not always appear, however. For example, on one of his television shows, Joel told viewers that they "are already victorious" and that "You have greatness in you" without any addendum that such greatness is to be used to benefit others.[21]

Silliman criticizes evangelical novelist Janette Oke on this point, namely, failure to assert that any abundance a believer receives is not just for that believer alone:

> She [the heroine of *Love Comes Softly*] received abundant life. But it was just for her and her family. There was no vision of common flourishing or care for the general welfare—abundant life was atomized, parceled out like suburban lots . . . .That woman was

---

17. Sinitiere, "Salvation with a Smile."
18. Bowler, *Blessed*, 134.
19. Bowler, *Blessed*.
20. Osteen, *Think Better*, 145.
21. August 23, 2020 (watched by author).

never asked to imagine how her abundance related to her neighbor's needs, or how her fullness and flourishing were bound up with that of other people. She was never asked to think of what it would be like to be part of a new community where her debts were forgiven as she forgave the debts of others.[22]

This message is very appealing. For one, it is completely compatible with American values. At least mythically or in our hopes and dreams, we see ourselves as positive people who believe in the American Dream: Work hard and you can become whatever you want to become. This goes beyond belief in God to belief in and commitment to hard work, but the optimism behind it is first cousin to the Prosperity Gospel. Parenthetically, the Prosperity Gospel flourished with the economic boom following World War II. The post-war boom offered confirmation that faith leads to economic well-being. At the same time, advances in medicine such as new vaccines (e.g., against polio) pointed to progress against disease.[23]

The Prosperity Gospel is not really new. It is basically a resurrection of the Gospel of Wealth espoused by such religious leaders as Baptist minister Russell Conwell and Episcopal bishop William Lawrence over a century ago.[24] Not surprisingly, the Gospel of Wealth was endorsed and practiced by steel magnate Andrew Carnegie. A major flaw of the Gospel of Wealth was that its proponents had little or no concern for social inequality and poverty, whereas the proponents of the Social Gospel highlighted the need for Christians to address social and economic reform. Osteen makes no mention of either of these two Christian outlooks on society and the economy, an indication of the superficiality of his message.[25]

Further evidence of the affinity of the Prosperity Gospel to the American mythology is Norman Vincent Peale's doctrine of the power of positive thinking. Peale preaches that positive thinking such as believing in yourself and building a mental picture of you succeeding and dismissing negative images of failure lead to success.[26] It is the Prosperity Gospel with belief in yourself replacing belief in God. It is interesting to note that President Donald Trump went to Peale's church and is a strong advocate of positive

---

22. Silliman, *Reading Evangelicals*, 213.
23. Bowler, *Blessed*.
24. Friedman, *Religion*.
25. For further details on the history of the Prosperity Gospel, see Bowler, *Blessed*.
26. Peale, *The Power*.

thinking.[27] Of course, it is a little easier to think positively when your father starts giving you what eventually amounts to millions when you are only two or three years old!

COMPARISON WITH THE MESSAGE OF JESUS

The problem with Prosperity Theology is that most theologians and church leaders do not believe that this Abundance doctrine is true. They see the message of Jesus Christ as a spiritual message that teaches love of God and love of neighbor and involves a heavenly reward rather than riches here on earth. In fact, they see Jesus as warning that it easier for a camel to pass through the eye of a needle than for a rich man to enter heaven (Matt 19:24). Also, they refer to the parable of Jesus in which a man lays up riches on earth—silos full of grain—and goes to bed unaware that he will die that night (Luke 12:13-21; note especially verse 15: "And he said to them, "Take care! Be on your guard against all kinds of greed; for one's life does not consist in the abundance of possessions.") Similarly Jesus told a rich young man that if he wanted to be perfect he should sell all that he had, give it to the poor, and come follow Jesus but the man could not bring himself to do that (Matt 19:21). Jesus also told the parable of the rich man who ate in lavish restaurants and ignored the poor Lazarus outside (Luke 16: 19-31). Based on these verses, Jesus does not appear to be someone who would tell his followers to go to Neiman Marcus, a Rolex store, or a Lexus showroom and celebrate one's birthday by lavishing money on themselves or their loved ones. As the Catechism of the Catholic Church puts it:

> It teaches us that true happiness is not found in riches or well-being, in human fame or power, or in any human achievement - however beneficial it may be - such as science, technology, and art, or indeed in any creature, but in God alone, the source of every good and of all love.[28]

Mitchell notes that even the non-canonical Gospels point to a Jesus that is not the abundance preacher of many televangelists. Mitchell argues that Jesus was very concerned that the rich not forget their obligation to assist the poor. In the non-canonical Gospel of the Nazoreans, for example, Jesus admonishes a rich man that he has not kept the Law and the prophets,

---

27. Blair, *How Norman Vincent Peale Taught*.
28. USCCB, CCC, 1723.

has not loved his neighbor as himself, as long as any persons "are dressed in filth and dying of hunger, while your house is filled with many good things and none of it goes to them."[29] And it appears that the early Christians took Jesus' teaching on riches to heart. In the Acts of the Apostles, we read:

> There was not a needy person among them [the early Christians], for as many as owned lands or houses sold them and brought the proceeds of what was sold. They laid it at the apostles' feet and it was distributed to each as they had need" (Acts 4:32, 34–35).

Biblical scholar Collins gives a cogent Biblical critique of the prosperity Gospel. He begins by noting that in the Old Testament keeping the commandments mainly centered on social justice. The Book of Job critiqued the notion that the righteous prosper by describing Job, "a paradigmatically righteous person who loses everything."[30] The Prophets spoke against the greed of entrepreneurs who grew wealthy by "exploiting the less fortunate."[31] In the New Testament,

> Jesus did not preach any form of a prosperity gospel, even one with deferred eschatological payout . . . .What we find consistently in the Gospels is an ethic of detachment, which depreciates the value of earthly goods. Luke 12:16–21 tells the story of the rich man who built new barns so that he had ample goods stored up for many years, but that very night God took his life. The rich man was not different from anyone who worries over a retirement account. He was only exercising the basic human instinct for self-preservation. The evangelist draws the lesson: "Be on guard against all kinds of greed, for one's life does not consist in the abundance of possessions" (Luke 12:15).[32]

So at least according to Collins, the Prosperity Gospel lacks a Biblical foundation.

GOD DOES NOT ALWAYS DELIVER WHAT YOU ASKED FOR

A major problem with the Prosperity Gospel is that God does not always deliver, at least not in the way the seeker might prefer. Prayer for a job, a

---

29. Mitchell, *The Gospel*.
30. Collins, *What Are Biblical Values?*, 187.
31. Collins, *What Are Biblical Values?*, 203.
32. Collins, *What Are Biblical Values?*, 203–4.

house, or a girlfriend or boyfriend does not automatically work. If you have a horrible disease like cancer, you may experience a miracle cure or you may not. Osteen implies that God *is* going to cure you. He does not spend much time talking about people who do not get cured but die from their disease. He implies that persistent prayer will get you that job, house, or money. Of course, Osteen can always tell believers who do not get what they want, "Don't give up. The answer to your prayer is just around the corner! Keep praying." But as cancer patient Kate Bowler wrote, I "can't outpray my cancer."[33]

Traditional theology suggests that suffering, such as suffering an illness like cancer, has redemptive value. Christ suffered the ultimate sacrifice of death on the cross. For many Christians, this is inspiration to endure their suffering, knowing that the reward of heaven awaits them. Traditional theology also teaches earthly material success is not the real goal of life. The real goal is to follow God in this life and get the reward of eternal salvation and heaven. When I was in a Catholic grammar school, the Baltimore Catechism asked, "Why did God make us?" And the answer was not the message of the Prosperity Gospel but: "To know, love, and serve Him in this world and be happy with Him in the next."

Prosperity preachers like Murdock do not give a damn, excuse the pun, about mainstream critics. Most objective viewers of televangelists such as Murdock, Tilton, and the like would question their sincerity and conclude that they want your money. Murdock's wealth is estimated at between five and ten million dollars.[34] Joel Osteen has a net worth of $100 million.[35] Granted, wealth is not intrinsically bad. It would be interesting, however, to see how much each of these wealthy celebrities has donated to charity.

Preachers such as Osteen are probably sincere. I think Osteen truly believes what he says. He just is not a theologian. He did not major in theology. He makes no mention of prior schools of thought such as the Gospel of Wealth or the Social Gospel. He picks his Bible verses and stories to reinforce his message that God wants all of us to prosper. Parenthetically, Osteen has achieved abundant success, both in terms of celebrity status, television ratings, book sales, and, of course, money, for his preaching. So

---

33. Bowler, *No Cure*.
34. *Insights Journal*, "Mike Murdock Net Worth."
35. Celebrity Net Worth Website, Osteen entry.

he can attest that the Prosperity Gospel has indeed worked for Joel (and his wife, Victoria)!

So a significant cadre of televangelists, past and present, preach the Prosperity Gospel. Some, like Murdock, appear to focus on wealth rather than the message of the Gospel. Others, like Joel Osteen, preach an amalgam of Norman Vincent Peale, Dale Carnegie, Horatio Alger, and other peddlers that offers abundance to those who believe, hope, pray, and, of course, make donations on their website. As Biblical scholar Collins points out, however, the message of Jesus is an ethic of detachment.

CODA: PROSPERITY GOSPEL REDUX: LET THE POOR EAT CAKE BUT ONLY IF THEY EARN THE MONEY TO BUY THEIR OWN CAKE

Some conservative Christian preachers have taken the Prosperity Gospel to the extreme. They proclaim that not only is it true that God rewards the righteous believer with prosperity, but they also contend that the poor are poor because they are lazy. And since they are lazy, the poor deserve no help from the prosperous believer. So prosperous believers have no obligation to feed the poor; no obligation to even offer them Marie Antoinette's infamous "cake." One such conservative preacher is John Hagee who has said: "America has rewarded laziness and we have called it welfare. [Whereas]] [t]he Bible says, 'the man who does not work, should not eat.'"[36]

These conservative Christians cite 2 Thessalonians where Paul urged the Thessalonians "to keep away from believers who are living in idleness" as Paul himself "did not eat anyone's bread without paying for it" and commanded his followers that "[a]nyone unwilling to work should not eat" (2 Thessalonians, 3:6–12).

Collins notes that these conservative Christians have erroneously cherry-picked the Bible for this one quote in 2 Thessalonians, whereas:

> In fact, the New Testament has a dominant position on the treatment of the poor. Feeding the hungry and taking care of those in need is a high priority for Christians. To be sure, there are abuses, which need to be addressed, but no person of goodwill can allow the occasional abuses to detract from the fundamental importance of providing for the poor as a biblical value.[37]

36. Quoted in Collins, *What Are Biblical Values?*, 210.
37. Collins, *What Are Biblical Values?*, 211.

THE PROSPERITY GOSPEL

So Prosperity Gospel extremists blame the victim (the poor) for their plight instead of following the Gospel mandate to help those in need. Recall the passage from the Acts of the Apostles (4:32, 34–35) noting the practice of the early Christians to help fellow Christians in need.

Thus the Prosperity Gospel appears to offer three courses of action vis-à-vis the poor. Hagee and company accuse the poor of being lazy and hence responsible for their own condition. So prosperous Christians owe them nothing except an admonition to stop being lazy. For preachers like Osteen there is the hint that abundance does carry some responsibility to help others. Similarly, Bowler focuses on the possibility of using abundance to help others:

> The money that the faithful come to possess was blessed because they who had it could do godly things with it—unlike the world's unfaithful who might use it in shameful or destructive ways.[38]

Bowler, however, seems to contradict this claim when she appears to justify Prosperity Gospel leaders' ostentatious displays of wealth (e.g., driving luxury cars) "as inducements to economic virtue...a path of prayer, frugality, and hard work."[39] This implies the third option: any abundance is simply for the believer or church leader, with no focus on helping others. This is Silliman's criticism of Oke's novels.[40]

To repeat something noted above, it seems hard to picture Jesus, were He here today, driving a Mercedes or a Lexus or living in a mansion or wearing thousand dollar suits. And the command to love your neighbor as yourself seems to suggest sharing rather than hoarding.

Parenthetically, many social scientists maintain that blaming the poor for being poor is simply bad science. They point out how our American economy contributes to if not causes poverty. An inadequate minimum wage, exorbitant housing costs, decreasing unionization, institutions such as pay day lending, consumer pressures to buy at cheap prices, the lack of national healthcare, and simple neglect of poverty in the midst of wealth all foster inequality and poverty.[41] So both the Gospel and many social scientists clearly agree that factors more complex than laziness are responsible for poverty in such a prosperous economy.

38. Bowler, *Blessed*, 234.
39. Bowler, *Blessed*, 235.
40. Silliman, *Reading Evangelicals*.
41. Desmond, *Poverty*.

CONCLUSION

On any given Sunday many Christians hear the Prosperity Gospel in a megachurch, a regular church, or on television. The extreme version can include alleged or proven con artists who appear to just want donations for their own pockets. The more nuanced versions include preachers such as Joel Osteen who read the teachings of Jesus to present a positive message of hope and expectation for abundance. That abundance can include financial and career success, health, and even healing.

Traditional theologians, however, interpret Jesus as calling for an attitude of detachment from wealth and action to assist the poor. A troubling aspect of the Prosperity Gospel is a number of preachers who go further and paint all of the poor as lazy individuals who by virtue of their sloth do not deserve any assistance.

One refreshing aspect of the Prosperity Gospel is that mainstream denominations do not endorse or preach it. The Prosperity Gospel often finds a home on television where proponents such as Joel Osteen spread its tenets. It is disturbing, however, that a poll showed that almost 40 percent of Protestants endorse it despite strong contrary messages in both the Old and New Testaments.

CHAPTER 3

Afterlife: Heaven and Hell: What Happens After We Die?

"Of course I'm pretty liberal; I don't exactly believe in a fire-and-brimstone Hell. Stands to reason, though, that a fellow can't get away with all sorts of Vice and not get nicked for it, see how I mean?"—George Babbitt (Sinclair Lewis)

She said, "I've been tramping around with the heathens. They're just as good as anybody, so far as I can see. They sure don't deserve no hellfire."—In *Lila* by Marilynne Robinson

"Singing hymns and waving palm branches through all eternity is pretty when you hear about it in the pulpit, but it's as poor a way to put in valuable time as a body could contrive."—Captain Stormfield (Mark Twain)

"Heaven is the ultimate end and the fulfillment of the deepest human longings and the state of supreme, definitive happiness."—CCC 1023

INTRODUCTION

TRADITIONAL TEACHING TELLS US we are all going to heaven or hell after death. Two features of hell are meant to "scare the hell out of us." First hell is eternal; second it is hell fire—a burning inferno that lasts forever. This is intended to frighten us into obeying the commandments and avoiding sin and (for Catholics) even "the near occasion of sin." Catholics also believe that many, if not most, believers need to experience a purification process—purgatory—before qualifying for heaven.

Hell and hellfire have been consistent staples of preachers and writers. Jonathan Edwards indicated that those going to heaven would enjoy heaven even more as they looked down on the damned: "The view of the misery of the damned will double the ardour of the love and gratitude of the saints of heaven."[1] In one sermon Edwards portrays not a loving God but a God who holds the damned in utter contempt:

> The God that holds you over the pit of hell, much as one holds a spider . . . abhors you, and is dreadfully provoked: his wrath towards you burns like fire; he looks upon you as worthy of nothing else, but to be cast into the fire.[2]

Very different from Edwards, contemporary televangelist Joel Osteen chooses not to preach on hell. He thinks people already feel guilty enough.[3] And, of course, hell does not seem like a fitting theme for the optimistic Prosperity Gospel.

While noting preachers on hell, it is appropriate to mention megachurch leader Rob Bell[4] since his questioning of hell prompted the Southern Baptist Convention to issue a reaffirmation of the doctrine of hell in 2011 (see below). Bell claimed that emphasis on hell subverted the Christian message of love, peace, forgiveness, and joy. Although he did not resolve the issue, he noted that universal reconciliation is one possibility. Although many Christians may not know it, this questioning of the existence of hell is know as universalism and its adherents claim it dates to the Church Fathers.[5]

THE TEACHING OF THE CHURCHES

The Catholic Church holds to a traditional teaching of hell, just like Jonathan Edwards:

1. Edwards, "The Eternity of Hell Torments."
2. Edwards, "Sinners in the Hands of an Angry God."
3. Kintz, "Joel Osteen Just Explained."
4. Bell, *Love Wins*.
5. Ehrman, *Heaven and Hell*.

> The teaching of the Church affirms the existence of hell and its eternity. Immediately after death the souls of those who die in a state of mortal sin descend into hell, where they suffer the punishments of hell, "eternal fire." The chief punishment of hell is eternal separation from God, in whom man alone can possess the life and happiness for which he was created and for which he longs.[6]

Similarly, the Episcopal Church defines hell as "eternal death in our rejection of God."[7]

After preacher and writer Rob Bell questioned the traditional teaching on hell, the Southern Baptist Convention issued a resolution in 2011 reaffirming its "belief in the biblical teaching on eternal, conscious punishment of the unregenerate in Hell."[8]

Evangelical Lutheran Church theologians Persaud and Fritschel write that hell is clearly part of Lutheran theology but they try to take some of the harsh edges off this depressing doctrine. They admit that after death hell is final but they attempt to soften any image of a harsh God who condemns us to hell by asserting that hell is more "a result of our own decision."[9] Despite the harshness of the doctrine of hell, they try to get Lutherans to trust in Jesus: "Through the Spirit, we are called to live in the gracious hope of what God has done for us in Jesus Christ. In that promise, we proclaim the good news, serve all people, and strive for peace and justice."[10] Translation: hell is depressing so let's not emphasize its proclamation.

Alexa Smith of the Presbyterian Mission Agency notes that she could only find one official Presbyterian statement about hell. That statement concluded that how God works redemption and judgment is a mystery. Thus,

> Hell has always been theologically troublesome, because it goes straight to the question of who God is: How do grace and judgment, or love and justice, mix in the divine mind? It is hard to talk about because this is hard stuff to talk about, but also because the Scriptures are not clear.[11]

---

6. *Catechism of the Catholic Church* (1035).
7. Episcopal Church, "Hell;"
8. SBC, "On the Reality of Hell."
9. Persaud & Fritschel, "Pondering Eternity."
10. Persaud & Fritschel, "Pondering Eternity."
11. Farinas, "What about hell?"

POLLING ON BELIEF IN HELL

Like Sinclair Lewis' George Babbitt, many Americans today do have questions about hell. While 91 percent of evangelicals say they believe in Hell, those percentages drop to 69 percent for mainline Protestants, 74 percent for Catholics, and 62 percent for all U.S. adults.[12] The easy explanation is denial; it is easier to deny the existence of hell than to avoid all the actions that might get you into eternal suffering. Or perhaps the doubters agree with scholars below who offer arguments against the traditional belief in hell.

HISTORIAN BART EHRMAN

Historian Bart Ehrman has written an entire book on heaven and hell. His first major proposition is that Jesus did not focus on heaven or hell but the imminent coming of the kingdom of God. Jesus preached a coming Day of Judgment with rewards for the just and destruction for those leading corrupt lives. Related to this, Ehrman asserts that Jesus "had no idea of torment for sinners after death."[13] The punishment for sinners is not hell but death versus life forever in God's kingdom for the righteous. For example, in Matthew, Jesus compares the day of judgment to fishing. "After fishing, the fisherman separates the good fish from the bad and simply throws away the bad. 'He obviously doesn't torture them.'"[14] Thus, Gehenna does not represent hell but simply the place where the evil will be destroyed. On the positive side, Jesus says "the coming Kingdom will entail a fantastic banquet where the redeemed eat and drink at leisure with the greats of the Jewish past, the Patriarchs."[15] Those hoping for sex after death, however, will be disappointed as those in heaven will be unmarried but, "presumably, eternally happy about it."[16] Ehrman asserts that Paul agrees with Jesus that nonbelievers will die and cease to exist, not go to a place of eternal torment.

Thus Ehrman states that the current teaching of Christian churches that sinners will suffer eternal punishment in hell is a later development. Ehrman also notes that in the 4th century some (e.g., Gregory of Nyssa)

---

12. Nortey et al., "Few Americans Blame God...."
13. Ehrman, *Heaven and Hell*, 155.
14. Ehrman, *Heaven and Hell*, 156.
15. Ehrman, *Heaven and Hell*, 161.
16. Ehrman, *Heaven and Hell*, 162.

taught that all will be saved. This is called universalism.[17] There will be suffering after death for sinners, but that suffering will annihilate evil. Thus, Rabbi Blech (see below) is not the first to state that perhaps hell is temporary, not permanent. Finally, Ehrman also notes that the notion of purgatory developed some centuries after Jesus as some thinkers thought that many believers are far from perfect and may need some preparation for heaven.[18] For the viewpoint that the traditional teaching on hell is biblical, see Young.[19]

Many Christians might disagree with Ehrman based on the story of Lazarus in Luke 16:19–31. This story seems to teach that the rich man is condemned to eternal torment in Hades. Ehrman disagrees; he argues that it is simply a lesson about how to live in relation to wealth. Ehrman also contends that this story was not told by Jesus but dates after Jesus' death. Ehrman's basis for this claim is that in the story the rich man asks Abraham to send Lazarus to warn his brothers. Abraham says there is no point in doing that because they would not believe even if someone were raised from the dead—demonstrating that this was written after the death and resurrection of Jesus.[20]

ALCORN: A TRADITIONAL VIEW OF HELL PLUS

Beyond stating that hell "will be a place of conscious punishment for our sins, with no hope of relief," Alcorn goes on to note the psychological aspects of hell: "Hell will be agonizingly dull, small, and insignificant, without company, purpose, or accomplishment....Hell and its occupants will exist in utter inactivity and insignificance, an eternal non-life of regret and—perhaps—diminishing personhood."[21] Although Alcorn claims to present a Scripture-based account of heaven, it is not clear which Scripture passages offer these particular psychological details about hell.

---

17. Ehrman, *Heaven and Hell*.
18. Ehrman, *Heaven and Hell*.
19. Young, *A Grand Illusion*.
20. Ehrman, *Heaven and Hell*.
21. Alcorn, *Heaven*, 27.

RABBI BLECH: A SOFTER, GENTLER VERSION OF HELL

Rabbi Benjamin Blech has an interesting take on hell. He believes that Jewish tradition and the insights of the Kabbalah do not teach the stereotype of hellfire and suffering. Bad news: hell does exist. Good news: it is not fire and brimstone. More good news: it does not last forever![22]

First, he argues that images of physical pain and torture are not accurate because we will no longer have physical bodies that can experience pain. So in heaven there will be no eating, drinking, or sex and in hell no excruciating physical pain. The pain of hell will be like the pain of disappointing our parents. As God reviews our life with us, we will experience the pain of disappointing a loving parent. "We grieve for our sins and feel intense pain for our failures. That pain, that self-inflicted hurt that comes from knowing how much we upset God by not living up to our divine potential, is the hell we have to endure for having messed up our lives."[23] Blech holds that the pain of hell is the realization one comes to after death that one has not lived the life one was called to live.

Second, Hell is not forever. It is a time-out for us to reflect on our lives and to repent and to renounce the wrongs that we committed. And this view means that when we have reflected and repented, then we can enter heaven. So hell is "a purification process" and the maximum term is twelve months!

Side Note 1: When I told a friend Blech's point about twelve months as the maximum time in hell, he responded, "So Hitler only gets twelve months!"

Side Note 2: So a Rabbi is basically offering the Catholic notion of purgatory!

HELL FOR A PHILOSOPHER: JOSHUA RASMUSSEN

Philosopher Joshua Rasmussen, who earned his Ph.D. in philosophy at Notre Dame, has written a recent book about how he, using a rational approach, journeyed from skepticism and doubt to, for him, the only rational conclusion: there is a foundation to the universe and that foundation is

---

22. Blech, *Hope, Not Fear*.
23. Blech, *Hope, Not Fear*, 100–101

God.[24] We will skip that interesting argument in favor of the existence of God to note Rasmussen's thinking on hell.

First, Rasmussen does not see hell as a place, like the prison Alcatraz, that God sends people to. Instead, he sees hell as separation from perfect goodness, i.e., God. On the one hand, if a person freely and continually chooses to distance him or herself from goodness, "then justice requires that their hell [their self-initiated separation from goodness] continue just as long."[25] On the other hand, he asserts that if the "ultimate purpose of hell—and of all perfect punishment—is to *purify*" then, "On this account, no soul stays in conscious torment endlessly."[26] He cites several theologians to support his thinking on hell.

So both an academic theologian and a philosopher (to repeat, a graduate of Notre Dame) who claims to have presented an essentially rational argument for the existence of God, have doubts about the traditional doctrine of hell as a place of eternal suffering (hellfire) from which no souls ever escape.

A PROGRESSIVE CHRISTIANITY DISCUSSION OF HELL

Progressive Christianity proponent Philip Gulley presents a picture of how he thinks Christianity needs to evolve to better comport with both science and reason. He argues that belief in both heaven and hell cannot be proven and that emphasis on either afterlife destination detracts from "those claims for which some proof does exist, such as the life of Jesus and his values, which ought to be the primary focus of Christian life."[27] In other words, Gulley thinks that emphasis on the afterlife influences us "to lose sight of the very life Jesus called us to live."[28] While Gulley's dismissal of both heaven and hell might seem extreme, note that N. T. Wright,[29] a more traditional theologian, has also called for less focus on the afterlife and more focus on participating in building God's kingdom in the present.

Another Progressive Christian, Brian McLaren rejects hell as a place of absolute agony or torment because his reading of the New Testament

24. Rasmussen, *How Reason Can Lead to God*.
25. Rasmussen, *How Reason Can Lead to God*, 172.
26. Rasmussen, *How Reason Can Lead to God*, 172.
27. Gulley, *The Evolution of Faith*, 199.
28. Gulley, *The Evolution of Faith*, 198.
29. Wright, *Simply Jesus*.

indicates that "the image of God that we see does not seem like an eternal torturer."[30] McLaren prefers to invite his listeners "to follow Jesus in a life of love for God and love for neighbors."[31]

CONCLUSION ON HELL

Traditional theology and preaching threaten believers with eternal damnation with severe suffering for serious sins. Many churches such as the Catholic Church and the Southern Baptist Convention continue to affirm traditional teaching on hell. Historian Ehrman claims that both Jesus and Paul envisioned *destruction* for sinners, not eternal damnation. Theologian Blech has a distinctly different view of hell, a purification process that involves psychological pain rather than physical pain. And it only lasts a year at most; that is the most that is needed to have remorse and repent. Philosopher Rasmussen, who has attracted attention for his rational defense of God's existence, sees God as perfect justice and perfect goodness, both of which attributes raise questions about such a perfect Being consigning humans to never-ending suffering and torture.

Clearly, scholars are raising serious issues with the concept of hell. Traditional teaching is meant to scare us away from sin and toward obeying the commandments. Just as the death penalty is meant to deter persons from crime, hell is meant to deter believers from sin.

Blech's view still has a hell but it is much less terrifying than the traditional version of hell. There is no hell fire and the maximum term is one year. Imagine the political reaction if a candidate for governor or president suggested that murder carry a maximum sentence of one year in prison! I doubt her campaign would survive. Theologically, Blech's viewpoint makes a great deal of sense. It fits with a view of God as loving and forgiving.

HEAVEN

In the story "Captain Stormfield's Visit to Heaven," Mark Twain raises some intriguing questions about what heaven might be like. The visitor expresses surprise that not everyone is wearing wings and carrying harps. The Captain's guide informs the Captain that the wings get heavy so quickly that

30. Kwon, "Interview."
31. Kwon, "Interview."

most inhabitants abandon them for the sake of comfort and mobility. Second, it is not simply Eternal Rest. There is work to do because "…as it is on earth—you've got to earn a thing, square and honest before you enjoy it."[32] Third, heaven is not exactly the same for every celestial citizen, as "I begin to see that a man's got to be in his own heaven to be happy."[33]

After noting the teaching of several churches on heaven, this chapter will discuss recent discussions of heaven by several theologians. Randy Alcorn offers the most detailed description of heaven, picturing it as the most luxurious resort imaginable! N. T. Wright, on the other hand, cautions against excessive focus on heaven versus emphasizing our part in God's re-creation of life right here and now. The discussion will also consider the issue of sex in heaven and the question of who goes to heaven.

THE TEACHING OF THE CHURCHES

The Southern Baptist Convention states that biblical revelation tells us about heaven, but does not expand on what that means specifically.[34] As the quotes above indicate, the Catholic Church asserts that heaven is a mystery but assures believers that whatever that mystery entails, the believer will be supremely happy.[35] The Lutheran Church-Missouri Synod teaches that heaven is a state of never-ending "blessedness" but adds that there will be grades of happiness: "there will be degrees of glory corresponding to differences of work and fidelity here on earth, producing praise to God but no envy (see 2 Cor 9:6; Matt 20:23)."[36] The Episcopal Church's *Book of Common Prayer* (862) describes heaven as "Eternal life in our enjoyment of God."[37] Its website expands that statement to "The unending fulfillment of salvation and happiness in relationship with God."[38] Methodists believe that heaven is God's dwelling place where believers will go after death and where they will experience freedom from sin and suffering.[39] The Presbyterian Church complicates matters with the doctrine of predestination: some

---

32. Twain, *The Complete Short* Stories, 611.
33. Twain, *The Complete Short* Stories, 607.
34. Southern Baptist Convention, "On the Sufficiency of Scripture."
35. USCCB, CCC, 1027.
36. Lutheran Church-Missouri Synod, "Frequently Asked Questions—Doctrine."
37. Episcopal Church, "Heaven."
38. Episcopal Church, "Heaven."
39. Joseph, "What Do Methodists Believe?"

are foreordained to heaven and some to hell. In fact, the concept of double predestination is "the belief that God creates some people whose purpose in existence is to be sent to hell."[40] We will forego discussion of predestination and focus on what heaven will be like.

WHAT WILL MAKE YOU HAPPY?

Given the statement in the *Catechism of the Catholic Church* that heaven is "the state of supreme, definitive happiness," a question is "How can that be? What will make you happy?" Here on earth it seems that we are never perfectly happy and that happiness is transitory. Yes, we are happy when work goes well, when family members are healthy and doing well in school, at work, and in their relationships. But it seems that we humans are always seeking new challenges, new tasks, new goals. As a recent retiree, for example, a major challenge of retirement is to find challenging, meaningful tasks.

As a college professor, each semester presented the new challenge of trying to get new groups of students to think and question and hopefully learn a bit about the subject of a particular course. Each year also presented the challenge of trying to write articles or books and get them published.

In retirement, those challenges of the workplace are gone. Similarly, years ago my wife and I faced the challenge and joy of raising two boys. Now that they are grown, they are facing their own challenges and do not need our assistance.

For anyone who golfs, he/she knows the constant challenge of the sport. So many things can go wrong with one's swing that the game is a constant challenge to get the swing right. Once in awhile, one has a great round; one seems to get in the "zone" where every shot is straight and far and putts go in the hole. But every golfer knows that the next round will not be that great and that is part of the lure of the game.

RABBI BLECH ON HEAVEN

Just as Rabbi Blech had much to say about hell, he also offers a view of heaven. First, we will not have our physical bodies in hell or heaven—so no sex, no eating, no drinking! The upside of his opinion is that hell will not

---

40. Got Questions Website, "What Is Double Predestination?"

be *physically* painful. The down side is that there will be no physical sex in heaven and, apparently, the "heavenly banquet" may not have any food or drink. The upside is that we will experience "indescribable happiness," via spiritual values, including the perfection of the intellect, but allowing for individual differences in each person's experience of heaven. [41]

Note that a sexless conception of heaven is not what some adherents of Islam have in mind, namely, that Islamic men will be rewarded with a number of virgins (*houris*) to offer sexual pleasure. Some believers reject this sexual interpretation and instead "interpret the idea of heavenly virgins as a metaphor for sublime satisfactions unimaginable on earth."[42] Still others, concerned about the sexist implications of a promise of virgins for deceased Islamic males, also interpret the metaphor in a nonsexual way or else say that women will also be offered sexual delights.[43]

ALCORN'S VIEW OF HEAVEN

While the Catechism of the Catholic Church observes that heaven is a "mystery...beyond all understanding and description,"[44] novelist and theologian Randy Alcorn has found enough words to write a complete book about heaven—the aptly titled *Heaven*. Since Scripture speaks of a "new earth," Alcorn proclaims that "we can expect to find earthly things there— including atmosphere, mountains, water, trees, people, houses—even cities, buildings, and streets."[45] He cites Revelation 21—22 as his source. He argues that we will have resurrected bodies, new bodies, and "...our destiny is to live forever on a restored and renewed earth."[46] And boredom will not be a problem: "Everywhere you go there will be new people and places to enjoy, new things to discover . . . . A party's ahead. And you're invited. There's exploration and work to be done—and you can't wait to get started."[47]

Alcorn even gets into a number of specifics about heaven. Bad news: no sex: "Because we're told that humans won't be married to each other, and

41. Blech, *Hope, Not Fear*.
42. Miller, *Heaven*, 83.
43. Miller, *Heaven*.
44. USCCB, CCC, 1027.
45. Alcorn, *Heaven*, 79.
46. Alcorn, *Heaven*, 91.
47. Alcorn, *Heaven*, 38.

sex is intended for marriage, then logically we won't be engaging in sex."[48] Good news: we won't miss sex. Although physical sexual intimacy will be missing, we will be experiencing fulfilling relational intimacy, which even on earth was the best aspect of sex. Also on the positive side, there will be privacy as "Scripture speaks of having our own individual dwelling place . . . (Luke 16:9)."[49] There is also a good chance that our beloved pets will join us in heaven. Not only will there be sports in heaven, but you will be able to play golf with Payne Stewart now and Tiger and Phil in the future—assuming Tiger and Phil make the cut to heaven. Or you can play catch with Andy Pettitte. Good books and good movies—those that do not celebrate sin—will be available. Travel will also be available, even to outer space.[50] Concerning bicycles, cars, and planes, Alcorn asks "why not?" There may even be time travel, that is, God allowing us to look in at past events as if they were happening in the present.[51]

A note about sports: Alcorn is not clear about some specifics. On the one hand, he asserts that heaven will offer us "continuous fulfillment of desires" but also "an eternity of learning and discovery."[52] If our desire is to break par in golf, continuous fulfillment suggests we will break par every time we play in heaven. But if we do that rather quickly in heaven, how will we experience "an eternity of learning and discovery"? In other words, if we have our desire to break par fulfilled rather quickly, won't we have learned how to play golf well rather soon after arrival? If so, it seems that we won't have much to learn and discover about golf very early in our stay in heaven!

N. T. WRIGHT: LESS EMPHASIS ON HEAVEN

Theologian N. T. Wright writes that many Christians have it all wrong if they think that the central point of Christianity is going to heaven or hell after death. Rather, the central question is "that of God's purpose of rescue and re-creation for the whole world, the entire cosmos."[53] In other words, Jesus was not discounting our present life on earth and "saving souls for a disembodied eternity but rescuing people from the corruption and decay

---

48. Alcorn, *Heaven*, 339.
49. Alcorn, *Heaven*, 38.
50. Alcorn, *Heaven*, 430.
51. Alcorn, *Heaven*, 433.
52. Alcorn, *Heaven*, 308.
53. Wright, *Simply Jesus*, 184.

of the way the world presently is so they could enjoy, already in the present, that renewal of creation which is God's ultimate purpose—and so they could thus become colleagues and partners in that larger project."[54] Wright asserts that Jesus has already begun the new creation. We participate in it whenever we do positive things, such as strive for justice and mercy. Wright is not as specific as Alcorn but he appears to be saying that earth will be transformed at the end time and heaven and earth will co-exist. Thus, Wright asserts that heaven and earth are "the twin halves of God's created reality, designed eventually to come together."[55] The start of this new creation is Jesus's resurrection such that "God's kingdom is now launched, and launched in power and glory, on earth as in heaven."[56] This kingdom is "a completely different way to live, a way of love and reconciliation and healing and hope."[57]

Wright is very vague about specifics. For example, given the millions of people who will have once lived on earth prior to the Last Judgment, one wonders where they, in their resurrected bodies, will all fit?

MILLER'S COMMENTS

Miller observes that modern life and conveniences, at least in countries such as the United States, offer people many goods, conveniences, and pleasures that people of old imagined they might one day see in heaven. As a result, "it's hard to convince people of a beautiful hereafter when in life they can buy almost anything they want."[58] On the other hand, in response to Mark Twain's concern about tedium in heaven, Miller echoes the Catholic Church's note that heaven is a mystery:

> "We don't know exactly what it will be like, they say, but it will be wonderful beyond our imaginings—not boring, certainly not ridiculous."[59]

Miller also notes the pronouncement of theologian N. T. Wright that heaven will be "like this present world, only much more so, its physicality

---

54. Wright, *Simply Jesus*, 192.
55. Wright, *Simply Jesus*, 193.
56. Wright, *Simply Jesus*, 193.
57. Wright, *Simply Jesus*, 194.
58. Miller, *Heaven*, 210.
59. Miller, *Heaven*, 219.

more real, its beauty more vivid, its pulsating life more intense and at the same time its peace more deep and rich."[60]

IS A PERFECT WORLD (HEAVEN) BORING?

In comments about earth, John Haught raises an issue about heaven. In responding to the atheists' argument that evil and suffering prove that an all-loving God cannot exist, Haught argues, to the contrary, that a perfect world would be boring and present no challenge. Instead of the imperfect world that we live in, "A morally acceptable God would get things completely right from day one. The universe would be an unblemished, unchanging refection of its divine engineer."[61] So Haught argues that human freedom to fight evil and imperfection and go through growing pains makes our lives interesting.

The problem for Haught is that he then needs to explain how heaven would not have the problems he sees with a perfect earth! He needs to explain precisely how a perfect heavenly world would not be boring but would present challenges, as challenges move humans to strategize, plan, and act. If a challenge is met, one feels a sense of accomplishment. So if a perfect earthly world would be boring because it lacks problems and challenges, how will a perfect heaven not have that precise problem of lacking challenge, change, room for growth—those aspects of earth that make it interesting?

Similarly, on earth we all experience the paradox that while we desire many things, often getting those things is not that satisfying. One example is Christmas. Hallmark movies and cable shopping networks want us to believe that a Christmas tree with a mound of presents underneath the branches will bring us perfect bliss. But on Christmas morning those presents, once opened, do not bring unending bliss. That shirt or piece or jewelry or even a new Lexus in the driveway all seem to lose the ability to satisfy very quickly. Likewise, when we were working, time off to play golf seemed like an idyllic retirement. In actual retirement, days without the demands and challenges of our former career may be harder to fill with meaningful and gratifying activity.

If heaven is playing golf everyday or a festive banquet everyday or meeting new saints everyday, that might not be happiness for everyone.

60. Quoted in Miller, *Heaven*, 220.
61. Haught, *God*, 106.

If there is indeed a heaven, I guess we will have to leave it to God to make heaven a place of love, peace, and happiness while at the same time dealing with how on earth we were motivated and energized by new challenges, new opportunities, new acquaintances, new tasks.

Perhaps the Catholic Catechism statement that heaven is a "mystery" is the best answer. Perhaps we just have to wait for our entrance to heaven to find out how we humans, who thrive on change and challenges, will find perfect contentment in a place that is outside of time and space and where perhaps all the physical pleasures we enjoyed so much on earth will give way to new pleasures in heaven.

SIDEBAR: WHO GOES TO HEAVEN?

It is interesting to note that Southern Baptists think they have an idea about who is *not* going to heaven. Over thirty years ago, for example, they estimated that 46.1 percent of Alabamians were unsaved and therefore risked going to hell. They reasoned that only those with beliefs matching the Southern Baptist faith would go to heaven, clearly ruling out Jews, Buddhists, and Hindus. But their criteria also excluded Catholics, prompting one Catholic to say he would start wearing a shirt "I'm one of the 46.1 percent!"[62]

In the discussion on hell, recall that Blech maintained that hell is only temporary: twelve months at most. So eventually all, including non-Southern Baptists, go to heaven. Recall also that philosopher Rasmussen agreed that hell is temporary because the purpose of punishment is purification. So Southern Baptists envision a limited population in heaven, while others see all going there. This calls to mind the old joke about Peter showing a new arrival around in heaven. Peter points out that certain groups—Baptists, Methodists, Catholics—are by themselves, because they think they are the only ones who qualified to get in!

CONCLUSION

Although not a theologian, Mark Twain clearly raised some critical questions about stereotypical views of heaven. Specifically, having wings and harps and singing hymns all day does not appeal to many of us. Thus

---

62. Washington Post, "Southern Baptists Take Heat."

Captain Stormfield's information that heaven involves both some form of work and also individualized pleasures seems more appealing. Not everyone likes the same things.

Alcorn offers a detailed vision of heaven that sounds like a five-star resort. For example, we may very well have pets, books, movies and even travel in heaven. To make up for the lack of physical sexual relations, Alcorn maintains that we will have the relational intimacy that, in his opinion, is the heart of sex on earth. Granted, relational intimacy is part of the joy of sex here on earth, but physical pleasure is certainly a basic component of sex on earth.

Wright agrees with Alcorn that heaven and earth will be part of the new creation started with the resurrection of Jesus but he does not go into all the details of heaven that Alcorn offers. Wright, instead, focuses on Jesus' message of a new creation that embodies love, forgiveness, and mercy now and in the future.

The safest answer seems to be that the question of heaven cannot be resolved. The Catholic Church said it best when it said that heaven is a "mystery." We have to wait for death and, hopefully, admission into heaven to find out what perfect happiness looks like. We will have to wait to find out how what perhaps made us happy here on earth will be matched by whatever makes us happy in eternity.

As far as hell is concerned, if Ehrman is correct that both Jesus and Paul taught that unbelievers/sinners are destroyed rather than suffer eternal torment, then people need not fear eternal torture, just annihilation or no afterlife. On the other hand, as far back as the fourth century some were saying that all will be saved. Sinners may suffer some temporary suffering but that suffering will cleanse them for heaven. Blech and Rasmussen offer contemporary versions of this positive view that an all-loving God does not consign persons to either destruction or eternal damnation. So one might follow Blech and Rasmussen to assure oneself that, at worst, there might be some temporary suffering for evil deeds but eventually all will enjoy heaven.

CHAPTER 4

Pre-Marital Sex: From Graduate School to Old Age

"Sexual relations outside of a biblically-ordained marriage between a natural-born man and a natural-born woman are not permissible at Liberty University."—Liberty University Online Honor Code

"If you believe that there is a God, a God who made your body, and yet you think that you can do anything with that body that's dirty, then the fault lies with the manufacturer."—Lenny Bruce

INTRODUCTION

MANY PREACHERS WILL NO doubt condemn premarital sex if they follow the formal teachings of their particular Church. For example, two of the largest denominations in the United States, the Catholic Church and the Southern Baptist Convention, officially state that sex is permissible only within marriage—traditional marriage between a man and a woman. As shown below, however, many Christians have concluded that that condemnation does not affect their personal decision to engage in such intimacy.

As noted in the discussion of homosexuality in Chapter 5, the Catholic Church's official position on sexual activity in general is that sexual intimacy is only permitted in marriage for heterosexuals.[1] And marital sex cannot simply be about the pleasure of the married couple. Sex also

---

1. USCCB, CCC, 2361.

involves a second end, the transmission of life. So sex has the twofold obligation of fidelity and fecundity.[2]

The Catholic Church addresses the issue of premarital sex under the traditional heading of *fornication*:

> *Fornication* is carnal union between an unmarried man and an unmarried woman. It is gravely contrary to the dignity of persons and of human sexuality which is naturally ordered to the good of spouses and the generation and education of children. Moreover, it is a grave scandal when there is corruption of the young.[3]

As noted in the discussion of homosexuality, the Catholic Church forbids all sexual activity outside of heterosexual marriage. Part of the reason for that condemnation is that the second justification for sex, for the Catholic Church, is openness to the possibility that sex leads to pregnancy.

In 1991 in Atlanta, Georgia, the Southern Baptist Convention felt pressure to react to onslaughts of relativism that were proclaiming that premarital sex was legitimate. Accordingly, the SBC adopted a Resolution on Human Sexuality which states that "Scripture condemns any abuse of sexuality, including premarital sex, adultery, rape, incest, pornography, promiscuity, prostitution, and homosexuality."[4] The Resolution also affirmed "the institution of marriage as the joining of a man and a woman."[5]

The Lutheran Church-Missouri Synod emphatically rejects premarital sex: "Sexual intercourse engaged in outside the marriage relationship is forbidden by the Scriptures and must be condemned by the church."[6]

POLL DATA

Before discussing theologians' writing about premarital sex, it is important to note public opinion on the issue.

In an October 2019 survey, the Pew Research Center found that 54 percent of mainline Protestants and 62 percent of Catholics stated that casual sex between unmarried adults is always or sometimes acceptable. In that same survey, 67 percent of mainline Protestants and 64 percent of

---

2. USCCB, CCC, 2363.
3. USCCB, CCC, 2353.
4. SBC, "Resolution on Human Sexuality."
5. SBC, "Resolution on Human Sexuality."
6. LCMS, "Human Sexuality," 12.

Catholics stated that sex between consenting adults in a committed relationship is always or sometimes acceptable.[7] The most recent statistic for all Americans, not broken down by religion, is that 76 percent of American adults say that sex between an unmarried man and woman is morally acceptable.[8]

All of these polls indicate that a significant percentage of Americans—over 75 percent in the recent Pew Poll—including significant percentages of believers, think that premarital sex is not wrong. This suggests that church teaching and preaching about this issue are not having the moral persuasion that they had years ago. While some who reject traditional teaching may simply be giving in to the desire for sexual pleasure, others may be concluding, as the arguments below say, that contemporary circumstances justify allowance for sex outside of marriage.

TWO THEOLOGIANS ON SEXUALITY

Two theologians have put forth arguments that contend that premarital sex is not only permissible but perhaps even praiseworthy! Knust makes the case that there is Biblical justification for such a positive view of premarital sex.[9] Peters uses theological reasoning to make the same case.[10]

Knust's Reliance on Scripture

Knust cites several references in the Bible that she claims allow for premarital sex. First, Exodus and Deuteronomy saw polygamy as the normal Israelite practice, and thus gave instructions regarding how to treat slave concubines and second wives. Second, the story of Ruth is a green light for premarital sex; she found food and marriage by sleeping with Boaz. Knust sees a similar lesson in the story of Bathsheba. Linking the two women's stories, Knust writes:

> ...passages celebrating sexual pleasure outside the bonds of marriage *can* be found in the Bible and, remarkably, no one dies. In fact, two of Jesus's ancestors risked the conception of children out

---

7. Diamant, "Half of U.S. Christians Say."
8. Brennan, "Americans Say."
9. Knust, *Unprotected Texts*.
10. Peters, *Trust Women*.

of wedlock—Ruth and Bathsheba—and yet neither these women nor their partners were killed. In these texts extramarital sexual expression leads to God's blessing, not God's curse, and sexual longing is both productive and positive. There is so much more to the Bible's teachings on sex and desire than current fearmongering suggests.[11]

Knust's final argument is that the Song of Songs in its entirety is an endorsement of eroticism that goes beyond conventional restraints:

> The frank eroticism of this poem, rare among the biblical books, suggests that the Bible's sexual mores can include sex outside of marriage. The Song of Songs, perhaps more than any other biblical book, refuses to be limited by common notions of "family values." Instead, this book celebrates pleasure for pleasure's sake.[12]

Hebrew scholar Renita Weems echoes Knust's citing of the Song of Solomon as a biblical endorsement of sex and sexuality when she refers to much of this biblical book as "eight chapters teeming with lust, love, sex, and passion in the middle of the Bible—and not once does the heroine or her beloved talk about marriage."[13]

The View of Peters

Peters argues that the traditional view that sex inside marriage is moral and sex outside of marriage is sinful is simplistic and erroneous. First, the traditional view assumes that a two-parent family is the best place to raise children. Peters states that this assumes that the purpose of sex is to have children and that a traditional family with husband and wife is the best way to raise children. Peters, instead, claims that "in our world today, most heterosexual activity does not produce children; nor does it have to."[14]

Next, she states that some Christian ethicists have advanced to focus on the quality of the relationship and why the partners wish to be intimate, including the issue of consent. Peters argues that the recognition of marital rape "recognizes the agency of women and affirms the belief that sex should

---

11. Knust, *Unprotected Texts*, Ch. 1.
12. Knust, *Unprotected Texts*, Ch. 1.
13. Weems, *What Matters Most*, 17–18.
14. Peters, *Trust Women*.

be consensual even within a marriage."[15] So the mere fact of the marriage relationship—a marriage license—is not what makes sexual intimacy moral. If it did, there could be no marital rape. What is critical is the quality of the relationship, including the consent of both parties.

Expanding on this point, she notes that a number of Christian ethicists have offered new, three-dimensional models of intimate relationships which focus on the equality of the partners:

> Three-dimensional ethical thinking looks beyond the surface configuration of a relationship (i.e., marriage) and asks challenging moral questions about the quality of the relationship, the behavior and attitudes of the partners toward one another, and why they wish to share physical intimacy. Questions like these offer a more rigorous ethical standard for sexual intercourse than a marriage certificate offers; an ethical standard rooted in the values of mutuality, justice-love, and right relation. Because Christian values, like all moral teaching, exist within particular cultural contexts, they must respond to those realities in ways that help interpret the core spiritual and moral values of the tradition in each age and place.[16]

So Peters' argument is that men and women can enter into relationships which are relationships of mutual love and that the partners in these loving relationships can also share sexual intimacy. The relationships, however, do not have to be limited to marriage.

Peters' view on relationships is very much compatible with Kant's practical imperative that we treat mankind as an end and never as a means. In fact, Marietta makes the point that "Today we see the view expressed by moralists who denounce exploitation of human beings as the only intrinsically wrong act."[17]

Surely, all of us can relate. All of us undoubtedly have had relationships where we really cared for the other person and they cared for us. And no doubt we have had relationships where we cared but the other party not so much, or vice-versa. Peters is saying that if the relationship involves two people who sincerely care for one another and both parties consent, sexual intimacy can be part of that relationship.

It needs to be noted that Peters and others who claim that premarital sex is morally permissible are not advocating casual sex at the drop of a hat.

---

15. Peters, *Trust Women*, 19.
16. Peters, *Trust Women*, 20.
17. Marietta, "On Using People," 232.

Unfortunately, it appears that many Americans have embraced extreme casual sex. Wade writes about the hookup culture on American university campuses. She observes that many college students are embracing this culture that endorses not only sex before marriage but sex before dating. She argues that many of today's students hookup immediately—engage in sex even before dating. As a result, many, especially the women, feel used because there is no feeling and no respect for the other party. Women feel like sex toys or simply body parts. If the male student sees the woman the next day, he does not even acknowledge her.[18] Peters is most emphatically not endorsing this hookup culture or casual premarital sex. She advocates for permitting sex for a man and a woman who are in love, respect each other, and are in some sort of committed relationship.[19]

Part of the reason for such an approach is that times have changed. Seventy-five or one hundred years ago, people graduated from high school—or not—and got married. They married at eighteen, or twenty-one or about that age. (And in Christ's time, they perhaps married at age sixteen!) Today, more and more young adults are postponing marriage to their thirties or even forties. Before marriage, however, they may have one or more long-term relationships. Peters is arguing that what is critical is how they treat the other person. If they just see the other as a sexual object—if all they want is immediate sexual gratification, then they are using that person and the premarital sex is not moral. But if both parties sincerely care for each other, then that is analogous to a marriage and the sexual activity is moral.

Note how she also dismisses the Catholic Church's emphasis on openness to conceiving a child by asserting that most sexual activity today "does not produce children; nor does it have to."[20] She is arguing that any focus on producing offspring is no longer a primary goal of most people who engage in sex today, married or unmarried.

TWO CONTEMPORARY SITUATIONS

Consider two contemporary situations that Jesus or the Church Fathers never faced. First, assume two law school students or two graduate students are in school in Chicago. They will be there for about three years. They have no idea where they will get a job after graduation. They date for awhile and

18. Wade, *American Hookup*.
19. Peters, *Trust Women*.
20. Peters, *Trust Women*, 19.

feel they love each other. Peters would argue that they can engage in pre-marital sex since they love each other and since they have a sound reason to postpone marriage. After graduation, one could wind up on the West Coast and one on the East Coast or one still in the Chicago area. So they think it is a good idea to wait before committing to marriage. The Catholic Church and the Southern Baptist Convention would say any such sex before marriage is sinful.

Another situation might be later-in-life "premarital" sex or simply sex without marriage. Assume two senior adults, aged fifty or older, both divorced or widowed. They meet and fall in love. Perhaps for legal or practical reasons they may not choose to marry. They both have good paying jobs or are retired and have respectable assets: investment accounts, retirement accounts, and so on. Perhaps they both have adult children and their own assets. Rather than get married and divide assets and draw up a will to stipulate which adult children get which assets in case of a death, they simply choose to live together. If they were twenty or more years younger and just starting out in life, they probably would have gotten married. But now with the complication (and blessing!) of assets, they simply choose to live together. So two major religious bodies would condemn their choice as sinful. But they see the choice as pragmatic.

The chapter on homosexuality (Chapter 5) cites Scripture Professor James Brownson for making the case that the Bible allows room for same-sex committed relationships. However, he also cautions that Biblical sexual ethics "includes, first, a rejection of promiscuity of all kinds and a deep valuing of committed love that cultivates and flourishes in lifelong relationships."[21] On the positive side, the Bible teaches that all relationships be both mutual and consensual.

So, it is clear that Brownson is not advocating one-night stands or exploitative relationships. His focus on "lifelong" relationships raises a question as to whether he would countenance the "graduate school" relationship noted above or a "senior citizen" relationship noted above. Speculation suggests he would be more favorable to two grad students who perhaps intend to marry but then change their minds and two seniors who also intend to marry but perhaps never "get around to it" or change their minds. In short, Brownson's emphasis on a *lifelong* aspect of a relationship limits which relationships he thinks meet scriptural approval.

21. Brownson, *Bible, Gender, Sexuality*, 267.

MOULTRIE: EROTIC JUSTICE

Moultrie also offers a picture of what moral premarital sex should entail. She writes that in her view "a womanist model of erotic justice is bodily centered and action-oriented toward justice. It focuses on self-pleasuring, oral and anal sex, and non-monogamous sexuality, asserting that instead of marriage as the ethical criterion of 'good and godly sex,' an emphasis on erotic pleasure and responsible sexuality should be normative."[22] Responsible sex includes several aspects. First, both partners need to be clear about the ground rules of the relationship, that is, "whether it's just about sex, sex and companionship, sex that is leading toward an exclusive relationship, etc."[23] Second, both partners need to know each other's STD and HIV status. Finally, Moultrie even allows for multiple partners as long as the above conditions are met. As can be seen, Moultrie takes a position that is considerably more expansive than that of Brownson and others.

ELLISON: A PROGRESSIVE CHRISTIANITY VIEW

Ellison rejects the traditional Christian sexual ethic which affirms only two possibilities: sex in heterosexual marriage or celibacy. He uses a 1991 Presbyterian Church USA study document which celebrates traditional marriage and also "all sexual relations grounded in mutual respect, genuine care, and justice-love."[24] So instead of Christianity endorsing a patriarchal view of sex, Ellison agrees with the Presbyterian study document that "a gracious God delight[s] in our sexuality and call[s] us to wholeness in community."[25] In such a Progressive Christian framework,

> good sex is defined less by the form of the relationship, for example, whether it is a marriage or even a heterosexual coupling, and more by the moral character of the relationship and whether it is constructed on the basis of mutual trust and respect, whether the parties are committed to a fair sharing of power and resources, and whether the relationship and its pleasures, as well as its

---

22. Moultrie, *Passionate and Pious*, 117.
23. Moultrie, *Passionate and Pious*, 136.
24. Ellison, *Making Love Just*, 33.
25. Ellison, *Making Love Just*, 32.

responsibilities and burdens, are equitably distributed and open to fair renegotiation as needed.[26]

So instead of emphasizing the "sin of sex," "a justice ethic of sexuality highlights the centrality of a responsible use of power, including erotic power, to enhance personal well-being and strengthen community ties of mutual respect and care across social categories."[27] Furthermore, sex is not limited to married men and women, but extends to the unmarried and persons of diverse sexual identities.

Parenthetically, the document was not adopted by the Presbyterian Church USA.[28]

MARRIED PERSONS WITH A SPOUSE WITH ALZHEIMER'S DISEASE: A SPECIAL CASE OF EXTRA-MARITAL SEX

Beyond asserting the right of single Christians to engage in premarital sex—as long as it fosters mutual trust and respect and justice—Ellison addresses the issue of sexual intimacy for a person whose spouse has Alzheimer's disease. His general directive is that the traditional teaching of sex only in heterosexual marriage or else celibacy is wrong.

As for the specific issue of one's marriage partner now suffering Alzheimer's and so the still healthy partner seeks intimacy elsewhere, Ellison maintains that the issue is not adultery or infidelity. Ellison, instead, sees the situation as one in which the Alzheimer's patient has abandoned his or her spouse:

> Granted, this abandonment is nonvoluntary, but it is the patient spouse who disappears, emotionally though not physically, and leaves the caregiving spouse. Subsequently, this becomes a story about the caregiving partner's moral wrestling about whether she is entitled to receive as well as give love, including the sexual love of a third party.[29]

If a caregiver chooses not to seek sexual intimacy with someone else, Ellison sees that as exemplary fidelity. Such extraordinary fidelity, however, is not the only ethical course of action. "In contrast, a life-giving ethic will

---

26. Ellison, *Making Love Just*, 33–34.
27. Ellison, *Making Love Just*, 34.
28. PCUSA, 1991.
29. Ellison, *Making Love Just*, 45.

encourage caregivers and, specifically, women to honor their own dignity and value and not discount their right to a personally fulfilling life."[30]

Clearly this is a predicament that did not exist in the time of Jesus or Paul. Life expectancies were much shorter. People did not live long enough to develop Alzheimer's. Given that Jesus and Paul did not address this matter, theologians and ethicists such as Ellison are attempting to fill in the gaps.

COMPARISON

Traditional teaching emphasizes the importance of marriage. It encourages people to commit to another person for life and to restrict sexual activity to a lifelong partner. Since the two parties pledge fidelity for life, each can be assured that the other party is not simply using them for simple sexual pleasure. Each party can rest assured that the other party cares for them for life. If children result from sexual activity, they have two parents who ideally will care for them and love them for as long as those parents are alive. And if both parties live into their senior years, each has the assurance of having someone to share their golden years.

One negative aspect of traditional teaching on premarital sex is that it forbids two people who may not be ready for marriage but who are in a serious relationship from expressing their love in sexual intimacy. As noted above, in the case of two graduate students who may be contemplating marriage, traditional teaching prevents them from sexual intimacy. A more liberal view, such as that of Peters, would allow these two hypothetical graduate students to engage in sexual intimacy. Similarly, senior citizens who are widowed or divorced may not want to marry for practical reasons but desire intimacy with another senior.

Going further, ethicists such as Ellison maintain that sexual pleasure is good not evil and even intimacy with no promise of a committed relationship is ethical. Ellison rejects traditional church teaching on sex as being both patriarchal and unjustifiably negative. He rejects traditional teaching that restricts sex to heterosexual marriage and mandates celibacy for the unmarried and for gay Christians (see also Chapter 5 on homosexuality).

A negative aspect of premarital sex, especially if it is on the frequent side, is that it can lead to sexually transmitted diseases and it can lead to unwanted pregnancy. An unwanted pregnancy can put pressure on the

---

30. Ellison, *Making Love Just*, 47.

couple to marry or to seek an abortion. Given one's view on abortion, the consequence of an unwanted pregnancy can lead to a second difficult decision, namely to keep or abort that baby.

As noted above, given longer lifespans and the prevalence of Alzheimer's disease, openness to premarital (or extramarital sex) can allow the caregiver of an Alzheimer's sufferer the chance to have an intimate relationship even though one's marriage partner is now mentally disabled.

CONCLUSION

Traditional preaching and teaching, such as that of the Catholic Church, the Southern Baptist Convention, and the Lutheran Church Missouri Synod, is that premarital sex is forbidden and sinful. Several current religious writers, however, argue that not only is it *not* sinful, it is perfectly legitimate. Knust uses the Bible to assert that several biblical writers affirm the legitimacy and even the beauty of sexual pleasure. Weems concurs with Knust about the Song of Solomon. Peters argues that today's circumstances argue for focusing less attention on marital sex and on intercourse leading to pregnancy. She notes that more people, married as well as not married, simply do not see sex as critically related to conception. Second, she argues that the recognition of the existence of marital rape—marital sex without consent—indicates that marriage itself is not the critical factor in assessing sexual morality. Consent is. Unmarried people can consent to have sexual intercourse or not. And the quality of the relationship is critical.

Peters also addresses the cultural context: Because Christian values, like all moral teaching, exist within particular cultural contexts, they must respond to those realities in ways that help interpret the core spiritual and moral values of the tradition in each age and place. So Peters claims that an ethical consideration of premarital sex would strive to "reflect equality and justice between partners."[31] Ellison concurs about a sexual ethic based on justice and he goes so far as to approve of sexual intimacy without commitment.

Traditional teaching such as that of the Catholic Church and the Southern Baptist Convention contends that the issue of premarital sex is a settled topic: it is clearly sinful. Recent writers, however, raise reasoned arguments that question that traditional teaching. It also seems that contemporary circumstances, such as two graduate students in a serious

---

31. Peters, *Trust Women*, 20.

relationship, two widowed seniors, or a spouse with a spouse suffering from Alzheimer's disease, present circumstances that did not exist at the time of Jesus. So a Christian can turn to very traditional teaching or can find a rationale for going beyond that traditional teaching.

CHAPTER 5

Homosexual Intimacy: Embracing Celibacy vs. Seeking Connection

"Every homosexual is potentially an evangelist of homosexuality, capable of perverting many young people to his sinful way of life." —Tim and Beverly LaHaye

"As a Christian I believe the Bible which defines homosexuality as sin, something to be repentant of, not something to be flaunted, praised or politicized. The Bible says marriage is between a man & a woman—not two men, not two women." —Franklin Graham (Tweet about Pete Buttigieg)

INTRODUCTION

MANY CHRISTIAN PREACHERS CONDEMN homosexual sexual activity. Catholic, Southern Baptist Convention, and Lutheran (Missouri Synod) preachers can turn to official church teaching that homosexual sexual acts are contrary to the law of God. An unique aspect of this position is that it tells gay persons that they, unlike heterosexual individuals, cannot engage in sexual intimacy. This chapter will discuss both the theological and personal aspects of traditional teaching.

The Catechism of the Catholic Church teaches that homosexuality as an "inclination" is "objectively disordered" and that "[h]omosexual persons are called to chastity." The Church encourages homosexuals to employ prayer and sacramental grace (e.g., Holy Communion and Confession) to "resolutely approach Christian perfection." To be fair, sexual intimacy is only permitted in marriage for heterosexuals. And marital sex cannot simply be about the pleasure of the married couple. Sex also involves a second end, the transmission of life. So sex has the twofold obligation of fidelity and fecundity.[1]

On October 21, 2020, however, Pope Francis offered his support for same-sex civil unions:

> Homosexual people have a right to be in a family. They are children of God and have a right to a family. Nobody should be thrown out or be made miserable over it. What we have to create is a civil union law. That way they are legally covered. I stood up for that.[2]

Then in December, 2023 Pope Francis again stirred up controversy when he authorized priests to give non-sacramental blessings to same sex couples. The blessings, however, cannot resemble a wedding in any way.[3]

On April 2, 2024, however, the Catholic Church released a Declaration on Human Dignity. On the one hand, this Declaration called for respect and considered treatment of all individuals, regardless of sexual orientation:

> The Church wishes, first of all, "to reaffirm that every person, regardless of sexual orientation, ought to be respected in his or her dignity and treated with consideration, while 'every sign of unjust discrimination' is to be carefully avoided, particularly any form of aggression and violence.[4]

On the other hand, the Church condemned sex change interventions.[5] More critically, it said nothing about changing the Church's position forbidding sexual intimacy for gay Catholics, let alone endorsing marriage for gay couples. Thus, as will be discussed below, the Catholic Church continues to cast gay sexual intimacy as sinful instead of recognizing the need and desire of all humans to enjoy such intimacy and to enter into a lasting relationship with one other human.

Similar to the Catholic Church, the Southern Baptist Convention claims that the Bible teaches that homosexuality is "a manifestation of a depraved nature," "a perversion of divine standards," and an abomination

---

1. USCCB, CCC 2358, 2359, 2361, & 2363.
2. Sherwood, "Pope Francis Backs Same-Sex Civil Unions."
3. Winfield, "Activists Hope."
4. Dicastery for the Doctrine of the Faith, *Infinite Dignity*, Paragraph 55.
5. Dicastery for the Doctrine of the Faith, *Infinite Dignity*, Paragraph 60.

in the eyes of God" (citing Lev 18:22; Rom 1:24–28; 1 Tim 1:8–10).[6] The SBC also claims that this "deviant behavior" has "wrought havoc in the lives of millions" and is "the primary cause of the introduction and spread of AIDS in the United States."[7] Despite these negative characterizations, the SBC offers consolation: "God loves the homosexual and offers salvation" such that "homosexuals, like all sinners, can receive forgiveness and victory through personal faith in Jesus Christ" (1 Cor 6:9–11).[8]

Similarly, the Lutheran Church-Missouri Synod states that the Bible "teaches homosexual behavior is contrary to God's will" and sees "homophile behavior as intrinsically sinful" and the "homosexual orientation is profoundly unnatural." The plan for ministry should be "to confront the individual with his/her sinfulness, and call him/her to repentance."[9]

On the other hand, the Presbyterian Church USA has issued formal statements allowing LGBTQIA+ persons to both serve in church ministry[10] and request a service of Christian marriage in states that allow same-sex marriage.[11]

In 2005, the United Church of Christ issued a formal statement in favor of the government allowing same-sex marriages and congregations not discriminating against same-gender couples:

> The Twenty-fifth General Synod of the United Church of Christ affirms equal marriage rights for couples regardless of gender and declares that the government should not interfere with couples regardless of gender who choose to marry and share fully and equally in the rights, responsibilities and commitment of legally recognized marriage;
> [The UCC bases its affirmation of same-sex marriage on] the life and example of Jesus of Nazareth [which] provides a model of radically inclusive love and abundant welcome for all.[12]

So if you are gay and a Catholic, a Southern Baptist or a Lutheran (Missouri Synod), you are called by faith to be "chaste." The quote from Franklin Graham above is indicative of preachers who follow such

6. SBC, "Resolution on Homosexuality."
7. SBC, "Resolution on Homosexuality."
8. SBC, "Resolution on Homosexuality."
9. Lutheran Church-Missouri Synod, "FAQS: Response to Homosexuality."
10. Matheson, PCUSA Votes."
11. NBC News, "Presbyterian Church (USA) Recognizes Same-Sex Marriage."
12. United Church of Christ. "Equal Marriage Rights for All."

church pronouncements. But a number of churches see no problem with homosexuality.

PUBLIC OPINION

Polling reveals that surprisingly high percentages of Americans in general and Christians, except evangelicals, favor allowing gays and lesbians to marry legally. Specifically, 61 percent of Americans, 66 percent of white mainline Protestants, 61 percent of Catholics, but only 29 percent of white evangelical Protestants favor this. Once again, significant percentages of believers support marriage for gay individuals contrary to official church teaching that preaches celibacy as the only path for gays to avoid sin and reach an afterlife in heaven. Finally, 79 percent of "nones" support same-sex marriage.[13]

THEOLOGIANS

We will look at what two theologians and one ethics professor have to say about homosexuality.

Focusing on the Bible, Collins emphasizes that Jesus and the Gospel writers are silent on this topic, "which should raise questions about the importance of homosexuality in the biblical world."[14] He notes the Pauline injunctions but asserts that they stem from the Hellenistic culture and Hellenistic Jews. Although Collins states that the Bible "provides no direct support for gay rights in the modern context" he also asserts that

> the explicit biblical condemnations of homosexual activity are confined to narrow strands of tradition in both Testaments. Modern discussions of gender and sexuality provide a very different context for this issue than is envisioned in the Bible. Many other considerations besides the few scriptural passages we have discussed would have to be taken into account in a responsible discussion of the ethics of homosexuality.[15]

For anyone seeking to find some biblical support for homosexuality and gay rights, Collins offers the suggestion "to argue from the general

---

13. Pew Research Center, "Attitudes on Same-Sex Marriage."
14. Collins, *What Are Biblical Values?*, 80.
15. Collins, *What Are Biblical Values?*, 81.

command to love our neighbor and would then have to face the difficulties of determining what love of the neighbor requires.[16] This suggestion does not take much imagination to follow. Homosexuals, like all humans, are our neighbors. Loving them would require treating them as our heterosexual neighbors. If we truly love them, we respect their sexual orientation and their need, their basic human need, to express that sexual orientation in intimate relationships.

New Testament professor James Brownson begins by noting that many traditionalists who see homosexuality as sinful use the argument that God intended the genders to be complementary, that is, different but matching, both physically and psychologically. Genesis 2:24 thus speaks of man and woman becoming "one-flesh" by bringing their complementary bodies and personalities to the marriage union. Brownson, however, claims that Scripture is *not* referring to anatomical or biological complementarity. Instead, the Bible is referring to kinship, which is based "on similarity and mutual obligation."[17] Second, he analyzes several Biblical references that seem to condemn homosexual behavior. He argues that these verses do not actually condemn homosexual behavior but sexual sins such as lust. For example, concerning Rom 1:24–27 he states;

> What is degrading and shameful about the behavior described in Romans 1:24–27 is that it is driven by excessive, self-seeking lust, that it know no boundaries or restraints, and that it violates established gender roles of that time and culture, understood in terms of masculine rationality and honor.[18]

Instead of lust, the Bible puts forth a positive sexual ethic focused on love and kinship:

> ...the Bible's understanding of the meaning of sexual relationships lies in the one-flesh kinship bond. This bond is formed when the desire for self-gratification (*eros*) comes to recognize that one's own gratification is only possible in the context of loving self-giving to the other (*agape*). Hence, longing turns to loving, as intimacy unfolds into long-term kinship bonds of service, commitment, and mutual care.[19]

---

16. Collins, *What Are Biblical Values?*, 81.
17. Brownson, *Bible, Gender, Sexuality*, 260.
18. Brownson, *Bible, Gender, Sexuality*, 218.
19. Brownson, *Bible, Gender, Sexuality*, 263.

Brownson addresses other biblical references to homosexuality. For example, he argues that the stories of Sodom and Gomorrah (Gen 19) and the Levite's concubine (Jdg 19) are actually about the horror of rape and the violation of male honor in rape. He notes that the prohibitions in Leviticus against "lying with a male as with a woman" were set in different contexts (pagan cults, Israel's role as a nation, etc.) and do not apply to contemporary committed same-sex relationships.[20]

Brownson concludes that the Bible does not condemn all contemporary forms of committed intimate relationships between same-sex individuals. This does not mean one-night stands or exploitative relationships but allows room for relationships that "are not lustful or dishonoring to one's partner, are marked positively by moderated and disciplined desire, and when intimacy in these relationships contributes to the establishment of lifelong bonds of kinship, care, and mutual concern."[21]

Christian Ethics Professor Marvin Ellison goes further than Professor Brownson. First, relying on William Sloan Coffin, Ellison simply casts aside biblical references condemning homosexuality as irrelevant "deadwood":

> Some of that [biblical] deadwood is about women, some about slavery, and still other is about homosexuality, which the Bible says little about and what it does say is either misinformed, plain wrong, or irrelevant to contemporary discussion about intimacy and covenantal love between two coequal partners.[22]

Second, Ellison argues that traditional teaching on sex has been completely negative; the only permissible sex is heterosexual, marital, and procreative. In other words, if one is single, one must be celibate because moral sex is limited to sex in marriage. Instead, Ellison calls for a new Christian sexual ethic that focuses "on making justice-love rather than procreative heterosexual marriage the normative expectation for intimacy and erotic exchange. This single relational standard calls for mutual respect and care, a fair sharing of power and pleasure, the maintenance of health, and, in those cases where it applies, the avoidance of unintended pregnancy."[23] As Ellison sees sexual pleasure as good, he does not mandate that it be limited to marriage or even to long-term commitments. He has no problem with

20. Brownson, *Bible, Gender, Sexuality*, 213.
21. Brownson, *Bible, Gender, Sexuality*, 277.
22. Ellison, *Making Love Just*, 66.
23. Ellison, *Making Love Just*, 70.

sexual dalliances as long as each party is honest with the other, respects the other, and just.

TRADITIONAL VIEW OF HOMOSEXUALITY VS. TRADITIONAL VIEW OF MARRIAGE

The Catholic Church mandates celibacy for gay Catholics, at the same time it endorses marriage for heterosexual Catholics. Citing Gen 2:18—"Then the Lord God said, "It is not good that the man should be alone; I will make him a helper as his partner" (NRSV)—the Catholic Catechism states that God calls humans to love: "God who created man out of love also calls him to love: the fundamental and innate vocation of every human being. For man is created in the image and likeness of God who is Himself love."[24]

So the Catholic Church officially teaches that "every human being" is called to the vocation of love but that gay Christians are forbidden from homosexual marital love. Gay Christians are prohibited from experiencing the mutual love and sexual intimacy that is at the heart of marriage—unless they somehow change identity to heterosexual and marry a person of the opposite gender.

This verse from Genesis and the Catholic Church, of course, are simply stating the sociological/psychological truth (see APA quote below) that each of us is a social animal. More than that, Gen 2:18 is affirming that we humans long for intimacy, that we seek an intimate and lifelong partner. So, Genesis shows God creating woman so that men and women need not be alone. But according to traditional Christians, God somehow does not care if gay men and women are forbidden to marry or to be intimate outside of marriage with one other human!

PSYCHOLOGY

Psychology professors take a completely different view of homosexuality. They see it as a normal sexual orientation. In response to the question whether homosexuality is a disorder, the American Psychological Association offers an emphatic "No":

> No, lesbian, gay and bisexual orientations are not disorders. Research has found no inherent association between any of these

---

24. USCCB, CCC, 1604.

sexual orientations and psychopathology. Both heterosexual behavior and homosexual behavior are normal aspects of human sexuality. Both have been documented in many different cultures and historical eras. Despite the persistence of stereotypes that portray lesbian, gay and bisexual people as disturbed, several decades of research and clinical experience have led all mainstream medical and mental health organizations in this country to conclude that these orientations represent normal forms of human experience. Lesbian, gay and bisexual relationships are normal forms of human bonding. Therefore, these mainstream organizations long ago abandoned classifications of homosexuality as a mental disorder.[25]

GAY VOICES

Since this is a quintessential personal issue, it seems appropriate to note what several gay writers are saying besides what scholars are saying.

In *A Change of Affection* Becket Cook recounts how a chance encounter with a gay Christian followed by a sermon on Romans Chapter 7 changed his life. At the time, Cook was living with another man. One Saturday while out for coffee with his partner, Cook encountered a gay person who believed homosexuality to be a sin and sincerely believed that "following Jesus was worth denying that part of himself."[26] Shortly thereafter, Cook heard a sermon that completely changed his conception of his identity, his purpose in life, and his understanding of God: "And I knew, in that moment, I knew into the core of my being that being gay was no longer who I was. But I didn't care. Like I had just met Jesus Christ."[27]

Similarly, Sam Allberry writes that he has come to realize that God is not anti-gay. God offers love and forgiveness, fullness of life, to all, straight and gay. Further, all believers must take up their cross to follow Jesus. All Christians are called to say "no to your deepest sense of who you are, for the sake of Christ."[28] Intriguingly, however, while heterosexual persons have to say no to sexual immorality—all sexual activity outside of marriage—they can say yes to sex in marriage. But since marriage is for a man and a woman, a gay man must give up his "deepest sense of who [he is] you are...

---

25. American Psychological Association, "Answers to Your Questions."
26. Cook, *A Change of Affection*, 6.
27. Banister, "Being Gay."
28. Allberry, *Is God Anti-Gay?*, 11.

for the very reason that your life, it turns out, is not yours at all. It belongs to Jesus."[29]

So a straight person might have to give up evils like envy, greed, lust for persons other than their spouse, gluttony, and so on. Christ is not anti-gay; Jesus simply wants a gay man or woman to give up sex altogether, to live a celibate life.

Imagine if Jesus or if Joel Osteen told their listeners that they have to relinquish all sex! That their only option is celibacy!! In 30 C.E. I can see thousands of Jews not waiting for the loaves and the fishes but fleeing the Sea of Galilee. In 2025 I can see thousands in the Compaq Center in Texas listening to Joel Osteen promise them thousands of dollars of prosperity (see Chapter 2 on the Prosperity Gospel) in their futures. But if he were to say "Give up sex; Jesus does not allow any sex in this life," I see those same thousands of listeners heading for the exits.

Allberry focuses on carrying your cross and saying no to the deepest sense of who you are. I think he has it wrong. I think God/Jesus wants us to develop and be the deepest sense of who we are. I think he wants us to seek to find what our talents are, grow them, and then use them. A dear friend of mine, also a now retired professor, and I have often discussed how we have felt blessed to be called to be college professors in a field that we love and with a chance to hopefully have an impact on the college men and women we had the privilege to teach. We never felt that we were carrying a cross or giving up who we were. We enjoyed teaching, were grateful for the opportunity, and felt that being engaged in teaching and research allowed us to express our abilities and our enthusiasm. [30]

Matthew Vines is a gay individual who presents scholarly arguments against traditional teaching. Consult his book[31] for those arguments, which echo both Collins and Brownson. However, unlike Cook and Allberry he cannot accept the position that God simply wants gay individuals to deny their very identity and to somehow live a life devoid of an intimate relationship.

Objection: sex is not necessary; Jesus was celibate. Vines:

> But as humans, our sexuality is a core part of who we are. It's part of what it means to be a relational person. Whether we ever pursue

---

29. Allberry, *Is God Anti-Gay?*, 11.

30. For more about both of our views of teaching as a vocation, see Braswell and Whitehead, *Teaching Justice*.

31. Vines, *God and the Gay Christian*.

romantic relationships, our awareness of ourselves as sexual beings and our longing for intimacy profoundly influence how we relate to others.[32]

Furthermore, Vines develops the suggestion of Collins to take Jesus's command to love one's neighbor. He notes that God has made us to be relational human beings and traditional condemnation of homosexual intimacy contradicts who we are as relational human beings and contradicts the injunction to love one's neighbor:

> Yes, plenty of Christian teachings are hard for us to live out. But no other teaching that Christians widely continue to embrace has caused anything like the torment, destruction, and alienation from God that the church's rejection of same-sex relationships has caused. If we tell people that their *every* desire for intimate, sexual bonding is shameful and disordered, we encourage them to hate a core part of who they were created to be. And if we reject the desire of gay Christians to express their sexuality within a lifelong covenant, we separate them from our covenantal God, and we tarnish their ability to bear his image.[33]

COMPARISON

If a gay Christian follows traditional teaching, he must embrace celibacy. The "Gay Voices" section above notes that this is possible, that some gay individuals come to believe and follow traditional teaching. Furthermore, they experience the love of God even though God commands them to be celibate. So traditional teaching such as that of the Catholic Church, the SBC, and the Lutheran Church-Missouri Synod offers a very conservative approach which sees homosexuality as disordered and sinful. As noted above, one wonders how this traditional view of homosexuality will persist or change in light of Pope Francis' recent comments on civil unions. At the very least, it appears that the Pope is no longer telling gay men and women that they must seek chastity and avoid all sexual intimacy. If one goes further, one could say that the Pope recognizes the need we all have for intimacy and is seeking a path for gay individuals to share intimacy and to express their love for another human being.

A non-traditional approach such as that of Brownson sees human relationships as essential for all, both heterosexual believers and homosexual

---

32. Vines, *God and the Gay Christian*, 155.
33. Vines, *God and the Gay Christian*, 158.

believers. Brownson argues that a gay believer can enter a committed relationship with another gay person without risk of going to hell simply because one is gay and craves sexual intimacy and commitment. Brownson does not approve of non-committed sexual encounters. Writers such as Peters (see Chapter 4) do see a place for premarital sex for heterosexual believers and, by extension, would most probably say the same for homosexual Christians. Writers such as Ellison go so far as to reject the traditional Christian sexual ethic and embrace sexual pleasure as ethically good even without commitment.

CONCLUSION

Many Christian preachers and official Church teaching in at least three major bodies (recall the Catholic Catechism, the Resolutions of the Southern Baptist Convention, and the position of the Lutheran Church-Missouri Synod) see homosexual relationships and sexual activity as inherently sinful. The message for gay Christians in these churches is that they are forbidden from entering into an intimate, committed relationship with another gay person. They must abstain from sex with any other gay individual. This teaching is based on several Biblical passages, especially Paul's letter to the Romans, 1:26–27. Going further, any hint of gay marriage is against the natural order created by God.

Other Christian denominations disagree on both homosexuality and on same-sex marriage. The United Church of Christ has issued a resolution for the government not to oppose same-sex marriage and exhorting UCC congregations to allow such marriages in UCC church settings. Similarly, the Presbyterian Church USA permits such marriages in their churches.

One development in this area is that Pope Francis has expressed support for same-sex civil unions and has ruled that priests can bless same-sex couples. While some see this as a possible harbinger of change, many Catholics see it as simply a call for compassionate pastoral care for gay Catholics.[34] On the other hand, a few Cardinals, including German Cardinal Reihnard Marx, have called for rethinking the Church's position on homosexuality.

Psychologists contend that the traditional view is simply not scientific. The American Psychological Association sees homosexuality as simply another sexual orientation, as simply one of several "normal forms of human

---

34. See, e.g., Dulle, "Explainer."

experience," as one of several "normal forms of human bonding."[35] So the APA would argue that the stances of the Catholic Church and the Southern Baptist Convention are bad science.

Some Christian Bible scholars, such as Collins and Brownson, argue that a wholesale condemnation of homosexual intimate relationships is simply wrong. First, it is based on erroneous interpretations of Bible passages. Second, it condemns gay Christians to lives devoid of intimate relationships even when God Himself is relational and has created humans to live in relationships. Collins argues that the Biblical condemnations of homosexuality are isolated and that Jesus and the evangelists had nothing to say on the topic. Furthermore, the context for the biblical passages is considerably different from today's context. Thus a contemporary discussion of the ethics of homosexuality needs to reflect "many other considerations."[36] Brownson agrees that the Biblical passages against homosexuality were set in contexts completely different from the contemporary context and that the Bible is open to same-sex relationships built on love and commitment.[37]

Ellison goes further than Collins and Brownson. Specifically, he argues that sexual intimacy and pleasure are positive goods and need not be limited to marriage, traditional or same-sex. So a man and a woman or two men or two women can choose to engage in sexual intimacy once, several times, for x length of time, or whatever. If they treat each other justly, sex is moral.

As noted above, Collins suggests that the general command of Jesus Christ to love our neighbor can be the starting point for an argument in favor of approving of homosexuality and even gay marriage. The Catholic argument (also cited above) that all humans are called to love and that marriage is a divinely ordained opportunity for humans to express and experience love suggests that gay Christians are also called to love and that they too should have the opportunity to experience love. Since we humans yearn to express our love physically as well as emotionally, intellectually, and spiritually, it seems logical to argue that gays can engage in physical intimacy and committed relationships. Otherwise, it seems that a church would be prohibiting gay Christians from the opportunity to express and experience love open to heterosexual Christians.

Changing from condemnation of homosexuality to acceptance and even approval would be a major step change for churches such as the

---

35. American Psychological Association, "Answers to Your Questions."
36. Collins, *What Are Biblical Values?*, 81.
37. Brownson, *Bible, Gender, Sexuality*.

Catholic Church, the SBC, and the Lutheran Church-Missouri Synod. However, churches have changed course on such matters as slavery, the death penalty, and on a patriarchal view of marriage. As noted above, the Presbyterian Church USA and the United Church of Christ have issued statements that are positive about homosexuality. Both of these churches think that a re-examination of the Gospel message in light of contemporary knowledge about homosexuality compels them to make the move from condemnation to approval. Also, several Catholic Cardinals have called for the Catholic Church to reevaluate its position on homosexuality and gay marriage. For example, Cardinal Reinhard Marx of Germany has stated that the Catholic Catechism is not "set in stone" after he was asked whether Catholics should regard an intimate relationship between two same-sex persons as "worthless."[38] As noted, above, in December 2023 the Pope authorized blessings for same-sex marriages. So there are indications that it is possible for Christian churches to change position on this issue. Perhaps it is time for all Christian churches to do the same.

A closing note is that conservative Christian thinking on homosexuality and gay marriage in fact seeks to go much further than simply condemning gay persons engaging in sex or getting married. Conservative Christian thinking also calls for additional restrictions on gay persons, some of which would affect many married heterosexual Christians. As Whitehead and Perry note:

> Threats to the "traditional" (patriarchal, heterosexual, nuclear) family are not just symptoms of sin in a fallen world. They are threats to the very fabric of American society. Consequently, the solution is not merely converting those souls to faith in Jesus Christ. The solution is the political reinforcement of godly order in covenant marriage laws, the elimination of no-fault divorce, constitutional amendments defining marriage as between a man and a woman, prohibiting homosexual or transgender persons from serving in the military, legislation that require persons to use bathrooms corresponding to their sex at birth, and protecting "religious freedom" to discriminate against sexual and gender minorities.[39]

---

38. National Catholic Register, "Cardinal Marx."
39. Whitehead & Perry, *Taking America*, 148–49.

CHAPTER 6

Divorce

"Divorce is never God's intention for our marriages. Divorce, according to the teaching of Jesus, is a concession to the fact and reality of sin in a fallen world."—American Lutheran Church

"The facility with which divorces are at present obtained in our courts is an incentive to exaggerate the minor difficulties of married life, and an encouragement to dissolve the union that otherwise would continue with difficulties removed."—Southern Baptist Convention

INTRODUCTION

DIVORCE IS A SIGNIFICANT phenomenon in the United States. The oft-cited statistic that 50 percent of marriages end in divorce, however, is inaccurate. Among ever-married adults 20 years and over, 34 percent of women and 33 percent of men have ever been divorced. The percentage of adults who have ever been divorced was highest (about 43 percent) for adults, male and female, ages fifty-five to sixty-four.[1]

Unlike the abortion issue, many churches recognize divorce as a fact of modern life and offer a sympathetic approach to their many members who have experienced one or even multiple divorces. This chapter will discuss the teaching of Jesus on divorce, the various approaches of churches to divorce, criticism of the Catholic Church's use of annulment to allow for

1. Mayol-Garcia, et al., "Number, Timing and Duration."

marital breakups, and a conclusion comparing the stance of churches on divorce to their positions on abortion.

DIVORCE IN THE NEW TESTAMENT

Collins notes that the views of Jesus on divorce are found in Matthew, Mark, Luke, and Paul. Specifically, both Mark and Luke say that divorce and remarriage constitute adultery based on Jesus' saying: "Therefore, what God has joined together, let no one separate" (Mark 10:9). Matthew, however, allows an exception for unchastity (5:32; 19:3–9). And Paul allows for divorce if a believer has married an unbeliever (the so-called Pauline Privilege). Collins argues that Matthew's exception is not the authentic teaching of Jesus: "The Markan and Lukan Jesus, however, allowed no exception, and one suspects that the more radical formulation is the more likely to be authentic."[2] Collins' final comment on what the New Testament has to say on divorce is that although the teaching of Jesus is quite severe, "many modern churches disregard the teaching of Jesus on this issue. Perhaps, like Moses, they make a concession to human weakness."[3]

Theologian H. Wayne House summarizes the Christian churches' positions on divorce into four possibilities: (1) neither divorce nor remarriage is permissible; (2) divorce is allowed but not remarriage; (3) divorce and remarriage are permissible in cases of adultery or desertion; and (4) Scripture decries divorce but God does not condemn those who divorce and remarry.[4] Grudem relies on I Cor 7:15 to argue that divorce is also permissible in further circumstances such as abuse.[5]

THE TEACHING OF THE CHURCHES

With this overview in mind, we will discuss the specific positions of select denominations.

The Catholic Church is an example of a church that categorically opposes divorce and remarriage based on the words of Jesus. According to the Catechism of the Catholic Church,

---

2. Collins, *What Are Biblical Values?*, 99.
3. Collins, *What Are Biblical Values?*, 99.
4. House, *Divorce and Remarriage*.
5. Grudem, *What the Bible Says*.

> Divorce is a grave offense against the natural law. It claims to break the contract, to which the spouses freely consented, to live with each other till death. Divorce does injury to the covenant of salvation, of which sacramental marriage is the sign. Contracting a new union, even if it is recognized by civil law, adds to the gravity of the rupture: the remarried spouse is then in a situation of public and permanent adultery.[6]

The Lutheran Church-Missouri Synod takes the following position:

> The Lutheran Church—Missouri Synod believes divorce is contrary to God's original design and intention for marriage. While divorce can be justified scripturally in certain situations (adultery or desertion), it is always preferable for couples to forgive and work toward healing and strengthening their marriage.[7]

The Southern Baptist Convention follows the third position noted above, divorce and remarriage permissible in cases of adultery or desertion, along with forgiveness for Christians who divorce for illegitimate reason but acknowledge their sin.[8]

In 1973 the Episcopal Church relaxed its stance on divorce. First, it recognized civil divorce. Second, it eliminated the previous one-year waiting period after divorce before remarriage could be considered. Third, it allowed for parish priests to make the decision to remarry, not a bishop.[9]

The United Methodist Church clearly states that divorce is regrettable but understandable and that remarriage is permissible:

> We recognize that divorce may become a regrettable but necessary alternative when marital relationships are strained beyond repair or become destructive or when spouses become irrevocably estranged. In such instances, we advise married couples to seek appropriate counseling and, if divorce proceedings become unavoidable, to conduct them in a manner that minimizes detrimental impacts on all family members.
>
> Fidelity to the marriage covenant does not require spouses to remain in a physically or mentally abusive relationship. We do not support efforts to withhold the church's ministries from divorced people or to deny them opportunities for leadership in the church, whether clergy or lay. We urge pastors and congregations

---

6. USCCB, CCC, 2384.
7. Lutheran Church-Missouri Synod, "FAQS: Family, Marriage and Human Sexuality."
8. Roach, "SBC not 'Third Way.'"
9. New York Times, "Episcopal Canon."

to provide ministries and programs that support divorced people in overcoming social and religious stigmas that they too often face. Divorce does not preclude remarriage.[10]

Given the frequency of divorce and remarriage in the United States, it seems safe to say that many Americans would be more likely to agree with the United Methodist Church rather than stricter positions. Public opinion research shows that 55 percent of American adults think that people stay in bad marriages too long while only 43 percent say that people get divorced too quickly. As expected, Democrats are more likely to say stay too long while Republicans are more likely to say divorce too quickly.[11]

THE CATHOLIC CHURCH AND THE ISSUE OF ANNULMENTS

A full understanding of the position of the Catholic Church on divorce requires a discussion of the Church's position on annulments. The Catholic Church has been criticized for condemning divorce and remarriage but permitting annulments. More specifically, the Catholic Church has been criticized for expanding the granting of annulments beyond the limited grounds that were relied upon in the past. In the past, non-consummation of the marriage was a reason for annulment. For example, if a couple could not physically have sexual intercourse, that marriage could be annulled. The Church could pronounce that the marriage never really existed because an essential element, sexual intimacy, could not be achieved.

In recent years the American Catholic Church has expanded the granting of annulments by focusing on marriage as a communion and by expanding the factor of defective consent. In other words, the American Catholic Church has come to see marriage as an ideal state between two individuals. If they divorce, their divorce then becomes evidence that either the man or the woman did not consent to try and bring about this ideal state of communion between the two parties. Vasoli argues that in the past and in Catholicism outside of the United States, the consent requirement is much simpler. The issue is whether at the time of the marriage the man and woman consent to a monogamous marriage for life; that they consent to restrict sexual intimacy to one another "until death us do part." He argues

---

10. United Methodist Church, "Social Principles."
11. Parker and Minkin, "Public Has Mixed Views."

that American Catholic clergy and canon lawyers have become so solicitous about divorced Catholics that they have misinterpreted some Vatican II documents and Papal instructions to see marriage as an almost unattainable ideal state and to see divorce as evidence that the parties did not actually have the requisite consent when they exchanged vows. He concludes that "[t]he American Church suffers a runaway tribunal system, bent on making annulment as easy and painless as possible."[12]

The impetus for Vasoli's examination of the Catholic Church's policy on annulments was his personal predicament. His wife of many years shocked him by deciding to seek an annulment of their marriage.

In support of Vasoli's contention that the Catholic Church has gone too far to grant annulments, there is a website called "Catholic Annulment: Another Chance" that informs Catholics how to start the process of requesting a church annulment. Revealingly, the website responds to the question whether a request for an annulment will automatically be granted as follows:

> Probably, but not necessarily. Any individual has the right to petition the Church for an annulment. This is very different from saying a person has a right to an annulment. The annulment process is contentious in church law, i.e., the marriage in question is presumed to be a valid marriage contract. So anything to the contrary has to be proven. The good news for you is that if you and you former spouse agree to cooperate in proving nullity of marriage, the process is much less contentious, and more likely to be granted.[13]

Vasoli would argue that this response of an annulment "probably" would be granted is evidence of the current Church's lax stand on annulments.

Vasoli meant to expose the annulment process in the Church. Critics might see the Church's position and practice as hypocritical. Critics might charge the Catholic Church with condemning divorce but then dissolving marriages via a distortion of annulment. Many people think that if one has been married for years—or perhaps decades—then that suggests that the marriage was consensual and valid. So the granting of an annulment appears very much a way to get around the teaching on divorce without saying that that teaching is erroneous or lacking.

---

12. Vasoli, *What God Has Joined Together*, 200.
13. Catholic Annulment Website.

ELLISON'S PROGRESSIVE CHRISTIANITY VIEW

As a Progressive Christian, Ellison disagrees that the problem is one of human weakness. He argues instead that traditional Christian sexual ethics has been "rigid, legalistic, and punitive."[14] Now, however,

> [a] more relationally focused ethical framework is called for, one that appreciates how the presumed ideal of lifelong, procreative heterosexual marriage no longer fits with, or speaks adequately to, our cultural reality. After all, divorce is not always tragic, but is sometimes the public recognition that an authentic marriage never took hold in the first place or at least has now ended for one or both parties.[15]

Further on Ellison quotes theologian John Cobb: "Protestants are becoming so accustomed to this acceptance of divorce and remarriage as the best response in many circumstances."[16] Intriguingly, Cobb notes that Protestants are accepting divorce and remarriage despite the fact that "it is Jesus himself who opposed divorce."[17] In other words, Ellison alleges that many Protestant churches are in practice adopting a Progressive Christianity approach to divorce.

It is also interesting to note that Ellison characterizes divorce as "sometimes the public recognition that an authentic marriage never took hold in the first place or at least has now ended for one or both parties."[18] That "an authentic marriage never took hold in the first place" amounts to the Catholic Church's position that annulments are allowed, that Church officials can rule that the marriage was not valid and can now be determined to have been invalid from the start. So a Progressive Christian theologian and the Catholic Church are essentially in complete agreement on this issue, except that Ellison would go further and say that the current cultural reality no longer fits with the teaching of lifelong marriage.

---

14. Ellison, *Making Love Just*, 4.
15. Ellison, *Making Love Just*, 4.
16. Ellison, *Making Love Just*, 15.
17. Quoted in Ellison, *Making Love Just*, 15.
18. Ellison, *Making Love Just*, 4.

A "PASTORAL" APPROACH

Shelly focuses on a pastoral approach to dealing with divorce. His deeper "reflection" on Jesus' teachings on forgiveness suggest a softer stance on divorce and remarriage than a literal rendering of the words of Jesus in Matthew, Mark, and Luke:

> With the God who has revealed himself in Jesus of Nazareth, repentance leads to real pardon and the opportunity to move on with one's life. Sometimes the emotional and spiritual mess is akin to scrambled eggs—eggs that can't be un-scrambled now. But there can be forgiveness and insight from past mistakes, and there can be normalcy in a new life. One can still marry and have a family. God deals with people redemptively. God's people need to do the same.
>
> A poor method of reading Scripture coupled with a lack of theological reflection has caused some people to believe sincerely that divorce is a sin worse than all others. Thus a person who quit trying in a marriage or one who destroyed a marriage by having an affair has been judged guilty of a sin for which there could be forgiveness, but it could not bring the option of a subsequent marriage. I once believed and taught this very thing, but I no longer think such a view represents either the heart or words of God as revealed in his Holy Scripture.[19]

Parenthetically, divorced and remarried Catholics are not supposed to receive the Eucharist at Mass. Many such Catholics, however, do receive Communion and many priests do not enforce the official teaching of the Catholic Church that they should not allow these Catholics to receive Communion.

Thus, the teaching of Jesus on divorce and remarriage is, on its face, quite strict. The Catholic Church, at least, continues to follow that teaching quite closely. Many preachers and Protestant churches, however, appear to disregard the teaching of Jesus on this subject. Even the Catholic Church opens a back door to divorce and remarriage by—according to Vasoli at least—broadening the grounds for annulment. So technically, the Catholic Church still abhors divorce. But it is rather generous in granting annulments, in saying that the original marriage was not in fact a marriage, so that a "remarriage" is actually the "first" marriage.

---

19. Shelly, *Divorce and Remarriage*, 14 & 18.

CONCLUSION: COMPASSIONATE VIEW OF DIVORCE VERSUS STRICT POSITIONS ON OTHER ISSUES

It is also interesting to compare the pastoral or compassionate approach of a number of churches to divorce versus the approach to homosexual intimacy and marriage and the issue of abortion. As noted, a number of churches are rather tolerant of divorce despite the severe teaching of Jesus. Recall Collins' position that both Mark and Luke, unlike Matthew, make no allowance for any exception to the edict of Jesus against divorce. Even the Catholic Church uses the back door of annulment to make allowance for its members who find themselves in a failed marriage. But many of these same churches make no allowance for gay Christians to feel ok about expressing intimacy in sexual activity or getting married. A number of churches simply admonish gay Christians to live celibate lives, lives devoid of a permanent intimate partner, unlike their heterosexual friends. Again, Jesus was very clear on divorce; he said it is wrong, either absolutely (ala Mark and Luke) or with minor exceptions such as adultery or abandonment (Matthew). On the other hand, he said nothing about gay marriage. So we have the situation of churches disregarding the explicit words of Jesus in Mark and Luke condemning divorce versus silence on gay marriage. And we have churches sympathetic to divorced and remarried Christians but allowing no room for gay Christians to enjoy the intimacy that all of us humans desire and need! One wonders if the passage of time will change this so that at some point in the future more churches will also take a "pastoral" approach to gay persons by downplaying any Scriptural or theological opposition to gay intimate relations and gay marriage. In other words, at some point in the future churches will blithely ignore past scruples about gay marriage and simply let gay members go about their lives in peace.

The so-called pastoral approach to divorced Christians also stands in relief to the position of conservative churches on abortion. They simply see abortion as wrong but they argue that human weakness makes it difficult for many Christians to stay married rather than get a divorce.

One might argue that the "pastoral" approach to divorced Christians that is sympathetic to the difficulties of marriage in the contemporary world might be a key to resolving the issue of inflexible stances on abortion, premarital sex, and physician-assisted suicide. Just as churches bend on the issue of divorce and remarriage, one could argue they should do the same with these moral issues. On divorce the churches seem to admit that we humans are far from perfect, that lifelong marriage in the twenty-first century is different from marriage at the time of Christ. For one, people are living into their seventies and beyond and a marriage of fifty years or more is not uncommon. If the churches were to be as sympathetic to persons facing difficult decisions about abortion, sex before marriage, and the suffering of one with a terminal illness such as ALS, perhaps they could envision that God is not as rigid as their pronouncements suggest. Perhaps God wants the churches to be as sympathetic to the human condition in areas beyond divorce and remarriage.

CHAPTER 7

Abortion: Two Meanings of Respect for Life, the Right to Choose, and the Lesson of the Good Samaritan Parable

"In the courts of heaven, abortion is murder in the first degree."—John Hagee

"Besides, every human being, even the child in the womb, has the right to life directly from God and not from his parents, not from any society or human authority."—Pope Pius XII

"The anti-abortion movement is using adopted children as its political football. The only moral solution to an unwanted pregnancy, this thinking asserts, is for women to do the right thing: carry the baby to term and relinquish the child for adoption."—Maria Laurino

INTRODUCTION

ROE V. WADE ENERGIZED many Christians to wage a war against abortion. That war led to the election of Donald Trump, his selection of three conservative Supreme Court Justices, and the *Dobbs* decision which reversed *Roe v. Wade*. The result is that red states have now banned most abortions and pro-life supporters are hoping to get federal legislation against abortion. Most Americans, including many Christians, however, continue to support abortion being legal in all or most cases[1] and pro-choice supporters say that *Dobbs* has energized them to elect legislators who are sympathetic to pro-abortion legislation.

Since Christians have led the fight against *Roe v. Wade*, it is critical to examine the pro-life arguments of churches such as the Catholic Church and the SBC, the nuanced positions of more liberal churches, and both theologians and other scholars who offer pro-choice arguments.

Pro-life advocates argue that the fetus is a person from the moment of conception. Hence, abortion is murder. The strongest advocates argue that the mother must carry the fetus to term even if the pregnancy is the result of a rape. Pro-choice advocates emphasize the right of a woman to make her own choices about reproductive health. They do not see the fetus as a human person from the moment of conception.

Independent of the debate over fetal personhood, women confronting the decision to abort face a variety of circumstances: their own health issues, possible fetal deformities, the effect of a pregnancy on their family, the impact of a pregnancy on their careers, and the presence or absence of a partner. If the pregnancy is the result of rape or the woman is under age 18, either of those factors can be critical.

This chapter will first consider the official positions of several major denominations on abortion as most preachers will follow the official position of their church. The next section covers opinion poll data on abortion. Then we will discuss several scholarly views on abortion, including those of two law professors and several theologians. The section will conclude with a discussion of how to resolve the differing stances on this critical issue of abortion.

HISTORICAL NOTES

In nineteenth century America abortion was not absolutely condemned. By the 1840s, many women were familiar with the ability of drugs to end a pregnancy. Although the law forbade abortifacients, women knew they could purchase these drugs from a doctor or druggist in person or through the mail. Opposition to abortion stemmed from fears that the practice was reducing the birthrate for white Americans while Catholics from Ireland and elsewhere and blacks were having more and more babies. Thus,

---

1. Pew Research Center, "America's Abortion Quandary."

Hostility to immigrants, Catholics, and people of color fueled this campaign to criminalize abortion. White male patriotism demanded that maternity be enforced among white Protestant women.[2]

A second historical note is that Protestants did not actively campaign against abortion until relatively recently. In 1968 the flagship evangelical periodical, *Christianity Today*, convened a group of about two dozen theologians who could not concur that abortion is sinful. In 1971, the Southern Baptist Convention passed a resolution allowing abortion under "a generous range of circumstances."[3]

WHAT THE CHURCHES SAY

Two major denominations, the Catholic Church and the Southern Baptist Convention, condemn abortion. The Evangelical Church in America, however, takes a more nuanced position. The basic pro-life argument is that life begins at conception, that the unborn child is a person, and abortion therefore is murder.

In the Catholic Church, the official position is that abortion is a grave sin, a mortal sin, because life begins at conception. The relevant *Catechism of the Catholic Church* paragraphs state:

> Human life must be respected and protected absolutely from the moment of conception. From the first moment of his existence, a human being must be recognized as having the rights of a person - among which is the inviolable right of every innocent being to life.
>
> Direct abortion, that is to say, abortion willed either as an end or a means, is gravely contrary to the moral law.
>
> Since it must be treated from conception as a person, the embryo must be defended in its integrity, cared for, and healed, as far as possible, like any other human being.[4]

The Southern Baptist Convention (SBC) has proclaimed that life begins at conception, that the unborn child is a person, and "repeatedly reaffirmed opposition to legalized abortion."[5] Consequently, the SBC sought

---

2. Reagan, *When Abortion Was a Crime*, Introduction.
3. Alberta, *The Kingdom*, 66.
4. USCCB, CCC, 2270, 2271, & 2274.
5. SBC, "On Celebrating."

the repeal of *Roe v. Wade*. In an earlier Resolution, the SBC equated legalized abortion with "genocide."[6]

It should be noted, however, that a few years prior to *Roe v. Wade*, the SBC had passed a resolution urging members to work for the legalization of abortion in circumstances of "rape, incest, clear evidence of fatal deformity, and carefully ascertained evidence of the likelihood of damage to the emotional, mental, and physical health of the mother."[7] And shortly after the *Roe* decision, a prominent Baptist leader, W. A. Criswell, praised the Court's decision and said abortion is not murder.

The Episcopal Church apparently allows for abortion in limited circumstances. On the one hand, the Church clearly does not embrace abortion for any reason: "we emphatically oppose abortion as a means of birth control, family planning, sex selection, or any reason of mere convenience."[8] On the other hand, the Church opposes legislation outlawing abortion. Instead, any legislation "must take special care to see that the individual conscience is respected, and that the responsibility of individuals to reach informed decisions in this matter is acknowledged and honored as the position of this church."[9] It appears that the Episcopal Church would allow abortion in situations such as when the health of the mother is in danger or possibly if the pregnancy is the result of rape, although the relevant Church document does not offer specific exceptions.

The Evangelical Lutheran Church in America (ELCA) takes a nuanced position which does specify several situations where abortion is possible. On the one hand, "in most circumstances, [it[encourages women with unintended pregnancies to continue the pregnancy."[10] On the other hand, the Church states that abortion is actually "morally responsible" where there is "a clear threat to the physical life of the woman."[11] Second, abortion is permissible in cases of rape and incest and in "some situations in which women are so dominated and oppressed that they have no choice regarding sexual intercourse and little access to contraceptives."[12] Third, abortion may

---

6. SBC, "On the Sanctity."
7. Cited in Griffith, 2017.
8. Episcopal Church, "Summary of General Convention Resolutions."
9. Episcopal Church, "Summary of General Convention Resolutions."
10. Evangelical Lutheran Church in America, "A Social Statement on Abortion."
11. Evangelical Lutheran Church in America, "A Social Statement on Abortion."
12. Evangelical Lutheran Church in America, "A Social Statement on Abortion."

be the responsible choice in "circumstances of extreme fetal abnormality, which will result in severe suffering and very early death of an infant."[13]

Similar to the ELCA, the Presbyterian Church USA has issued a statement both affirming respect for life and also respecting a woman's right to choose in "problem pregnancies":

> The considered decision of a woman to terminate a pregnancy can be a morally acceptable, though certainly not the only or required, decision. Possible justifying circumstances would include medical indications of severe physical or mental deformity, conception as a result of rape or incest, or conditions under which the physical or mental health of either woman or child would be gravely threatened.[14]

Once again, examination of the official positions of several Christian churches shows that sincere Christians can and do differ on critical issues. Two major bodies condemn abortion while the Episcopal Church respects each woman's individual conscience and the Evangelical Lutheran Church in America goes so far as to call abortion "morally responsible" in one situation and "permissible" in others. The Presbyterian Church USA states that abortion can be a "morally acceptable" decision in problem pregnancies.

POLL RESULTS

Before we discuss what theologians say about abortion, it is critical to note that a majority of Americans and many believers say that abortion should be legal in all or most cases and that *Roe v. Wade* should *not* have been overturned. Specifically, a Pew Poll found that 62 percent of all Americans, 61 percent of white non-evangelical Protestants, 71 percent of black Protestants and 60 percent of Catholics support abortion being legal in all or most cases. On the other hand, 73 percent of white evangelical Protestants think that abortion should be illegal in all or most cases.[15] And 83 percent of religiously unaffiliated Americans think it should be legal in all or most cases and 57 percent of all Americans disapprove of the Supreme Court decision to overturn *Roe v. Wade*.[16]

---

13. Evangelical Lutheran Church in America, "A Social Statement on Abortion."
14. Presbyterian Church USA, "Abortion/Reproductive Choice Issues."
15. Pew Research Center, "Broad Support."
16. Blazina, "Key Facts."

The Catholic percentage favoring abortion is noteworthy in light of the clear and direct teaching of the Catholic Church on abortion. The Catholic Church not only officially condemns abortion, but it strongly supports Right to Life efforts such as demonstrations outside abortion clinics and public marches against abortion.

Similarly, a recent Gallup Poll indicates that 69 percent of Americans think that abortion should generally be legal in the first trimester of pregnancy; 37 percent legal in the second trimester; and 22 percent even in the last three months. Over half (52 percent) of all Americans consider abortion morally acceptable. A clear majority (61 percent) think that overturning *Roe v. Wade*, was a "bad thing."[17]

An earlier Gallup Poll indicated that 48 percent of Americans consider themselves pro-choice and 46 percent pro-life. However, on the specific question of the morality of abortion, 47 percent think it is morally wrong versus 44 percent who think it is morally acceptable. Concerning the legality of abortion, 50 percent think it should be legal in only under certain circumstances, 29 percent legal under any circumstances, and 20 percent illegal in all circumstances. The category "certain" circumstances breaks down to 14 percent "most," 35 percent "only a few," and 1 percent "unspecified" circumstances. The author of the report concluded that "Americans' views on the legality of abortion are not evolving but staying roughly where they have been for nearly half a century."[18]

The fact that the Pew poll found that 62% of Americans think abortion should be legal in all or most cases did not affect the Supreme Court which recently overturned *Roe v. Wade*. Note that law Professor Steven Calabresi had contended—erroneously—that "the Supreme Court will not overrule incorrect or immoral decisions when the public clearly opposes doing so."[19]

DWORKIN

Dworkin was not a theology professor but a law professor, and now deceased. He presents an interesting argument, namely, that the debate over abortion is often misguided because it focuses on the wrong issue. Specifically, he thinks that the debate often appears to be about life or respect for life and it appears that the two sides have no room for compromise.

---

17. Saad, "Broader Support."
18. Saad, "Americans' Abortion Views."
19. Calabresi, "How to Reverse," 85–92. See below for more on Calabresi.

Opponents assert that the fetus is a person and that respect for life prohibits "murder" of a person. Proponents of abortion argue that the fetus is not a person and therefore there is no issue of murder; instead, proponents assert the right of the woman to choose.

Dworkin argues that respect for the sanctity of life does not necessarily involve asserting the personhood of the fetus. He claims that respect for the sanctity of life involves two aspects. One aspect is that to end any life prematurely is tragic. But a second and also critical aspect about the sanctity of life is that we humans care deeply about the investment each of us makes in his or her life.[20] In other words, each of us wants to live a life that we are proud of, a life that involves each one of us putting effort into it so as achieve something of meaning and to relate to others. A paradigm is someone getting an education, choosing a career, working years in that career trying to accomplish worthwhile goals, choosing a marriage partner, having and raising children, and so on. In other words, life is not just a biological fact. All of us want our life to mean something; we want to make something of the gift of life.

Dworkin argues that one reason for an abortion might be that a woman is in college and striving to become some sort of professional. If she were to have a child, that might end her plan and dream to become a doctor, lawyer, teacher, professor, or whatever. It would thwart her plans to invest herself, her hopes, energy, and hard work into her life, to make something of her life.

So respect for the sanctity of her life—respect for her hopes and plans to make a life for herself and for others—can and should allow for her to choose to have an abortion. An abortion shows her respect for life, that is, her investment in and commitment to living a meaningful life. Concerning the unborn child, Dworkin would argue that the woman thinks she does not have the ability to properly care for and raise the child at that time. So she is concerned that she could not invest properly in that unborn child's life.[21]

Dworkin also makes several important points to address critical issues. He notes that liberals but also many moderate conservatives do say that abortion should be allowed to save the life of the mother. He argues that if the fetus is really a human person, then this is tantamount to killing one person to save another and that is not allowed. He also argues that

20. Dworkin, *Life's Dominion*.
21. Dworkin, *Life's Dominion*.

even some conservatives would allow for abortion if the fetus was created by an act of rape or incest. Again, if these conservatives truly believed, says Dworkin, that the fetus is a person, they would not allow for any exceptions.[22] Of course, some pro-life advocates are so absolute about their position on the life and personhood of the fetus that they brook no such exceptions.

Conservative Law School Professor Steven Calabresi, on the other hand, disagrees completely with Professor Dworkin. Calabresi has called abortion "a loathsome procedure" and *Roe v. Wade* "not merely wrongly decided" but "also profoundly immoral."[23] In the article where he wrote those statements, he does not explain the reasons for his opinion except to note that he is pro-life and in favor of "the protection of the unborn."[24] Interestingly, he had argued that the Supreme Court would not overturn *Roe v. Wade* if public opinion were strongly on the other side. Thus he outlined a strategy for changing public opinion from favoring the legality of abortion to opposing abortion. As we now know, however, the Supreme Court overturned *Roe* despite public opinion.

What is noteworthy for our purposes is that Calabresi, like Dworkin, a prominent law school professor, apparently takes the pro-life position that a fetus is a human person and takes it so strongly that he calls abortion "loathsome" and "profoundly immoral." Given that position, it is difficult to imagine that Dworkin could win Calabresi over to his argument that respect for the sanctity of life (as defined by Dworkin) can be used to justify abortion. So we have two law school professors arguing very different positions on abortion.

MCGLASSON ON ABORTION

McGlasson takes what can be called a middle view: he agrees that abortion is wrong but he thinks that the evangelical crusade against abortion has three problems. First, he thinks any position against abortion needs to be balanced with concern for the mother. Second, he argues that if Christians are so concerned about life, they should be in the forefront in the fight for healthcare:

22. Dworkin, *Life's Dominion*.
23. Calabresi, "How to Reverse," 85.
24. Calabresi, "How to Reverse," 92.

ABORTION: TWO MEANINGS OF RESPECT

If life in all its forms is precious, then why are evangelicals not the *first in line* to promote every reasonable effort to extend healthcare to everyone? After all, the Bible is filled with miracles of healing; if God's inbreaking rule brings healing in its wings, why don't evangelicals make healthcare for all citizens—for all humanity—the *one highest priority* of their political existence?[25]

Third, he argues that to be consistent, Christians who oppose abortion also need to oppose capital punishment: "Capital punishment is a crime against the gift of life. Yet why are evangelicals not making the *end of capital punishment* the one litmus test for deciding upon a candidate."[26] The Catholic Church, of course, is one body that opposes both abortion and capital punishment (see Chapter 9 on the death penalty.)

A side note is that McGlasson also claims that evangelicals politicized this issue in 1980, eventually making it a litmus test for voting. One consequence is that evangelicals supported former President Trump in considerable part due to his opposition to abortion and his promise to appoint Supreme Court justices who would vote to overturn *Roe*. (He appointed three conservative Supreme Court Justices.) Watching political ads shows that most conservative candidates focus on clearly proclaiming support for the Second Amendment and for the pro-life position on abortion.

Similar to McGlasson, sociologist Andrew Whitehead, who also declares himself a devout Christian, calls for Christians to not limit their ethics to the abortion issue:

> I hope for the day when American Christians advocate just as vehemently for racial reforms to the housing, education, poverty, health care, and criminal justice systems as we have for the sanctity of life for the unborn.[27]

COLLINS AND THE QUESTION OF BIBLICAL VALUES

Focusing on what the Bible has to say about abortion, Collins writes: "There is no explicit discussion of abortion in the New Testament."[28] Collins argues that the "long history of Christian condemnation of abortion" dates to Tertullian who in the 2nd or early 3rd century CE likened abortion to "quicker

25. McGlasson, *Choose You*, 113.
26. McGlasson, *Choose You*, 113.
27. Whitehead, *American Idolatry*, 157.
28. Collins, *What Are Biblical Values?*, 55.

murder."²⁹ The condemnation does not come from the New Testament, nor does approval. So "the Bible does "not affirm either the fetus's right to life or the mother's right to choose."³⁰ Collins hypothesizes that perhaps abortion was not practiced very much in Old Testament circles or at the time of Christ. So, for "whatever reason, the biblical authors apparently did not see it as a problem that required explicit comment."³¹

This lack of biblical condemnation or endorsement is noteworthy. Protestants rely on the Bible as their guide for doctrinal and moral beliefs. As noted in the section on capital punishment, for example, the Southern Baptist Convention uses both Old Testament verses and Chapter 13 of Paul's Letter to the Romans as its justification for supporting the death penalty. On the other side, the Catholic Church has recently cited several passages from Matthew on forgiveness (including the Lord's Prayer, Matt 6:12), as at least part of their rationale for now opposing capital punishment.³²

One final word on Collins: he reiterates that "the Bible does not say anything directly about the subject (of abortion)," and "At the very least this should warn us that abortion is not a central concern in the Bible, and it certainly cannot be a litmus test for biblical values."³³ So, like McGlasson, Collins thinks that the recent tendency to judge political candidates solely on their position on abortion is not biblical and, thus, not Christian.

PETERS ON ABORTION:

Peters takes a much more direct stance: abortion is not only justifiable in cases such as rape or incest. Instead it is a moral decision based on the rights and dignity of women and based on the status of the prenate. Parenthetically, she titles her book as a "progressive Christian argument for reproductive justice" but she never explicitly explains how her thinking is indeed a progressive Christian argument.³⁴

Contrary to pro-life advocates who argue that life begins at conception, Peters argues that the prenate is in the process of becoming a human being but is not there until birth. She prefers to use the term prenate instead

---

29. Collins, *What Are Biblical Values?*, 56.
30. Collins, *What Are Biblical Values?*, 58.
31. Collins, *What Are Biblical Values?*, 56.
32. USCCB, "Statement on Capital Punishment."
33. Collins, *What Are Biblical Values?*, 58.
34. Peters, *Trust Women*.

of fetus or embryo to emphasize that there is not a baby, a human person, until later in development. She notes, for example, that the shell, if you will, looks more like a baby when an ultrasound is taken but that the internal development of the prenate takes much longer than the baby-like appearance on an ultrasound screen suggests. Peters sees the prenate as "dependent on a woman's [the mother's] body for life. Until they have drawn breath, expanded their lungs, and activated all their own vital bodily functions—prenates are utterly dependent and utterly *not-yet*."[35]

Thus, for Peters, there is a fundamental difference between the prenate and the just born infant:

> The prenate is fragile, contingent, potential, not-yet. Its very existence is fluid, in all the senses that that word encompasses—adaptable, unpredictable, changeable, unstable. It lives in a protective sac buoyed and secured by fluid, and its developing lungs are filled with fluid. It does not breathe until it enters the world. With this first intake of breath, the prenate crosses that threshold from nascent or potential life into the world of the living....Something happens when a child emerges into the world and takes its first breath and the umbilical cord is cut. Something shifts when the prenate moves from absolute biological dependency on a female body that transforms it from prenate to infant."[36]

Theologically, she argues that theologians and religious leaders have mistakenly relied on misinterpretations of Genesis to posit that the fundamental role of women is to bear children and be mothers. She similarly attacks Christian writers for painting women into three slots. Women can only be mothers, virgins, or whores. Mary, the mother of Jesus, is the ideal woman because she became a mother via a virgin birth, thus avoiding the messy matter of engaging in sexual intercourse with a man.

Peters contends that the focus on the prenate as human from conception and the focus on women's role as being a mother distort the abortion debate. She sees the issue as women having the right to decide what to do if and when they become pregnant. She notes that birth control is far from perfect; 50% of women seeking an abortion had ben using birth control. Furthermore, contraceptive methods are not perfect. For example, over a ten-year period with typical use the failure rate for diaphragms is 72 percent.

---

35. Peters, *Trust Women*, 131.
36. Peters, *Trust Women*, 161.

Abortion, however, is never an abstract ethical question. It is, rather, a particular answer to a prior ethical question: "What should I do when faced with an unplanned, unwanted, or medically compromised pregnancy?" This question can only be addressed within the life of a particular woman at a given moment in time. When a woman is faced with this ethical question, her answer will vary depending on the individual and the many factors—social, economic, personal, religious—that define her life at any given point.[37]

Peters argues that women should have the right to decide if they are able to have a child. Some women end their pregnancies because they think that they are not capable of having a child (or another child). Thus, "only the pregnant woman is in a position to know if she is ready, willing, and able to continue a pregnancy and to mother a(nother) child."[38]

KAMITSUKA

Margaret Kamitsuka has written a comprehensive book on abortion that disputes the pro-life arguments against abortion and in their place presents a pro-choice theological ethic.[39] The interested reader should consult this work for a complete discussion of abortion. Here we will simply note a few critical arguments.

Kamitsuka devotes considerable ink to discussing the main pro-life argument: that the fetus is a person from the moment of conception. First, she argues that pro-life advocates incorrectly cite Genesis to argue that since God created humans in the image of God the fetus is a person since it is formed in the image of God (*imago Dei*). Kamitsuka argues that the concept of creation in the image of God is not a core concept in the Hebrew Bible. Second, she argues that it would be a "massive hermeneutical leap" to infer that the Genesis creation stories "should be applied to human beings in the womb."[40] Those stories referred to adults. Then she notes that instead of explaining how an unborn is a "person," some pro-life thinkers now say that the unborn from conception on contains the *blueprint* for what eventually will be a person. So even some pro-life advocates themselves see the

---

37. Peters, *Trust Women*, 6.
38. Peters, *Trust Women*, 172.
39. Kamitsuka, *Abortion*.
40. Kamitsuka, *Abortion*, 54.

difficulty of maintaining that an embryo or a fetus is a person in the same way that adult individuals are persons. Finally, she explains how pro-life advocates erroneously downplay the importance of the gestating mother and write as if the fetus in the womb is an autonomous individual. Current science is instead emphasizing the critical role of the gestating mother for the developmental processes necessary for fetal development. In summary, "an embryo or developing fetus...cannot continue to exist apart from its gestating mother. Gestation is not just temporary nutritive dependency analogous to a hospital patient on a feeding tube or connected to a ventilator. The fetus is a developing human being uniquely interconnected with its mother, within her body."[41] Going further, Kamitsuka argues that the fetus has value but "the only person authorized to make the momentous decision to abort is the gestating mother."[42]

Another highlight of her work is an entire chapter devoted to the parable of the Good Samaritan. Kamitsuka begins by detailing how pro-life advocates use this parable to argue their case. They argue that just as the Good Samaritan sacrificed for the good of the man waylaid by robbers, so also both the pregnant woman and believing Christians should come to the aid of the unborn fetus when its mother is contemplating an abortion. First, the mother should not have an abortion but instead, like the Samaritan, think of the welfare of the endangered fetus. Pro-lifers go so far as to maintain that the woman has a duty to birth the child. Second, Christians should try to help women contemplating abortion with financial aid and social support. Pro-life advocates give examples of churches giving considerable aid and support so that the women chose to keep their babies.

Kamitsuka first notes the glaring weaknesses in the pro-life interpretations of the Good Samaritan parable. While the Samaritan did act ethically and even beyond the call of duty, the money he gave to the innkeeper to care for the victim of the robbery was only one day's wages, plus a promise to pay more if necessary. Even if he had to give more on his return, it would amount to only monetary aid. Pro-life advocates, on the other hand, are demanding that a woman endure nine months of pregnancy with all the normal pains of that pregnancy, the pains of childbirth, and a lifetime of maternal care. As anyone can see, what the Samaritan did, as praiseworthy as it was, is nothing comparable to what pro-life advocates demand the woman to commit to. Additionally, Kamitsuka argues that pro-life

---

41. Kamitsuka, *Abortion*, 106.
42. Kamitsuka, *Abortion*, 153.

advocates basically treat a pregnant woman as the donkey or mule that the Samaritan put the victim of the robbery on. Just as that donkey or mule had no choice in carrying the burden—the victim—from the site of the crime to the inn, pro-life Christians give the woman no choice but to carry the fetus to term and then care for the born child for a lifetime.

Kamitsuka then offers a modern Good Samaritan parable in which a sheriff sees a pregnant woman in trouble, offers to take her to a Planned Parenthood office, and even gives her money but says she should do what she decides. Such a scenario recognizes the situation the woman is in and also respects her agency and freedom to make her own choices about having a child and choosing maternal responsibility for life or not.[43] A final comment is that the reliance of pro-life advocates on the parable of the Good Samaritan is clearly an example of going beyond the original intent of the Gospel writer. To repeat Collins' appraisal: "There is no explicit discussion of abortion in the New Testament."[44]

We do not have room to summarize Kamitsuka's entire book. We simply note that she addresses Paul's views, the views of the Church Fathers such as Tertullian and Augustine, Biblical issues, philosophical issues, scientific issues, and feminist concerns, including detailed responses to several pro-life scholars.

ELLISON

Ellison argues that Christian tradition has not always seen protection of fetal life as an absolute value. Ellison notes that both Augustine and Aquinas did not equate abortion with homicide until ensoulment took place, marked by fetal movement. So the Church has not always been focused on protecting fetal life. Instead the motivation was "worry that abortion would cover up illicit sexual activity, especially nonmarital sex."[45]

Ellison believes that emerging fetal life is indeed valuable, but there are other values in play, including the mother's "own well-being, her duty to protect her own health and life, her right and need to pursue her own life plan, and her need to pay attention to current obligations that she feels bound to fulfill, including responsibilities to children already born."[46]

43. Kamitsuka, *Abortion*.
44. Collins, *What Are Biblical Values*.
45. Ellison, *Making Love Just*, 109.
46. Ellison, *Making Love Just*, 102.

"Because competing claims require their attention, women are obligated to exercise their freedom as moral agents and make conscientious choices about whether to continue a pregnancy or not. Procreation is, therefore, properly situated within a zone of moral freedom, discernment, and deliberation."[47] Factors involved in such choices include "the health and well-being of the woman, her circumstances, and the presence or absence of community resources."[48]

He goes on to argue that abortion needs to be seen as an issue of justice. He notes that there is an "appalling lack of justice for women in so many areas of their lives."[49] Women of color, for example, experience the social injustices of widespread poverty and racial hierarchy.

There is also the reality that current normative sexual practice is contracepted sex, not sex to have children (procreative sex). So in the United States most "women typically want and have two children and then spend roughly three decades trying to avoid becoming pregnant."[50]

> To counteract past injustices and patriarchal bias, the church and its majority male leadership must now declare their resolve to defend women's moral and legal right to birth by choice and also fearlessly advocate for public policy that reflects this commitment. Given the reality of an unjust world and the significant constraints most women encounter in their sexual and reproductive lives, the ethical principle that should guide us in these matters is a shared commitment to promote reproductive justice for all women, especially those marginalized by race and class disparities rather than "mere" advocacy for the far more elusive freedom, at least for most women and men, to exercise something called unfettered choice. In the best sense of the word, being "pro-choice" should mean taking a robust stand on the side of justice for women and investing one's life energy to help create a world of far greater equality and respect for women's well-being and bodily integrity. a world which we do not yet inhabit, but the vision of which sparks our religious and moral imaginations as a good worth living and struggling for, together.[51]

---

47. Ellison, *Making Love Just*, 102.
48. Ellison, *Making Love Just*, 105.
49. Ellison, *Making Love Just*, 105.
50. Ellison, *Making Love Just*, 108.
51. Ellison, *Making Love Just*, 144.

GUTMAN AND MORENO

Bioethicsts Gutman and Moreno state that the crux of the abortion debate is the question of when a fetus becomes a human person. They contend that this debate is "impossible" and "is not resolvable by reason alone."[52] But they argue that one way out of this unresolvable argument is for pro-life parties to accept that their position is 100 percent logical and true for them, but they have to admit that others may see their position as contestable. If there can be a reasonable doubt about their position that life begins at conception, then pro-life adherents should respect a woman's right to choose since one cannot prove the pro-life position to that woman.[53] Of course, conservative churches and traditional scholars do not accept the conclusion of Gutman and Moreno that the question of personhood is unresolvable. Kaczor, for example, offers a strong case for the pro-life position in general and for the specific point that individual personal life begins at conception.[54]

COMPARISON

Traditional teaching offers extensive protection for the unborn child [prenate]. If all abortions were illegal, all unborn children [prenates] would be born, all life would be protected. Another positive aspect of the pro-life position is that it resonates with the positive feelings of couples who have just found out that the woman is pregnant and with scholarly arguments on the pro-life side. These couples feel that their "child" is alive and growing and pro-life scholars argue that human personhood begins at conception. On the negative side, some unwanted children would be born with unknown psychological consequences. Many women would probably accept and love their children and raise them with love. But if parents are ambivalent or negative about having a child, their parenting may be less than optimal. Another negative aspect of abortion is that its availability may contribute to the hookup culture discussed in Chapter 4. Both men and women may be more willing to engage in premarital sex knowing that if a pregnancy occurs as a result, abortion is possible. They do not have to get married or bring up a child. Also on the negative side, many women may have their

---

52. Gutman and Moreno, *Everybody Wants*, 61.
53. Gutman and Moreno, *Everybody Wants*.
54. Kaczor, *The Ethics of Abortion*.

plans for their careers or for their children (families) they already have disrupted or forever thwarted. A woman in graduate school or a mother who already has three children may find a first or an additional child to be beyond her capacity to cope. Finally, some unknown number of children will be born into families that cannot necessarily afford them. Pro-life proponents might argue that economics is not as important as parental love and that many outstanding citizens grew up in less than ideal economic circumstances.

The positive side of a position such as that of Dworkin, Peters, or Kamitsuka is that women would not feel guilty about having an abortion but would instead feel respected as autonomous adults free to make a choice they think is best for them. These authors do not think the aborted prenate is really a human being so there would not be guilt about killing a "child." The negative side is that even if the positions of Dworkin, Peters, or Kamitsuka came to be accepted by many, there undoubtedly will always be traditional Christians who see abortion as murder. Witness the number of Christians who have protested abortion clinics! Those traditional views can continue to have residual effects on women who choose abortion. Another negative side of a pro-choice position is that some women may choose abortion when perhaps a decision to have the child would be the better decision for them. Perhaps in the stress of finding out that one is pregnant when the woman is experiencing other stressors in her life, she may choose abortion when perhaps having the child would have been a wonderful experience for her. This last scenario comes with the caveat that the issue is for the woman to decide and it can easily be presumptuous for someone else to suggest to any woman that the outsider knows what is best for her.

ADOPTION: A FALSE ALTERNATIVE

Pro-life advocates state that adoption is a positive alternative to abortion. In addition to allowing the fetus to live, it saves the woman from having to raise the child. It offers the child a loving home with parents who really want the child. It offers couples or single persons who cannot bear children a chance to have a child. Pro-life advocates are even going so far as to encourage states to legalize and provide safe haven bay boxes where mothers can drop off a newborn without any fear of criminal prosecution.[55] Parenthetically, Justice Alito noted the recent passage of "safe haven" laws

---

55. Laurino, "Unwanted Infant."

in several states as a recent development cited by pro-life proponents as one argument against abortion: a woman can use this option instead of abortion. Going even further, Justice Amy Coney Barrett suggested that states could require women to carry fetuses to term since the mother could legally abandon the newborn to a safe haven box!

What pro-life advocates do *not* note is that adoption is not as positive as traditionally assumed. First, if the adoptee never learns the identity of her birth parents, she is blocked from knowing her medical history. Second, at some point in their lives many if not most adoptees come to a feeling of having been abandoned by their birth mother. Abandonment is at the heart of the adoption process: a woman decides not to keep her baby. Related to this is the issue of closed versus open adoption. In a closed adoption it will be difficult for the child to ever find his or her birth mother and natural father. Various databanks make it easier to find one's birth mother but it can be a difficult task. Also, dropping off a baby at a safe haven baby box makes it impossible for an adoptee to ever discover her parents.

If the adopted child is nonwhite and the parents are white, the child may never have a chance to interact with members of her own race. The child may be prevented from growing up knowing what it means to be black or Hispanic in the United States. Recall the television show *This Is Us* as an example.

Finally, international adoptions make it hard for an adopted child to know what it means to be Korean, for example, if the child is Korean and the parents are American. Further, an international adoption makes it much more difficult, if not impossible, for the adopted child to eventually discover and meet the birth mother.

Another basic problem with adoption is that the "vast majority of women denied access to abortion do not want to give up their child."[56] Research indicates that if denied access to abortion, about 9 percent of mothers give up their child for adoption and 91 percent parent the child

This does not mean that all adoptions are tragic. It does suggest, however, that not every adoption is automatically positive. It points out difficulties that can arise in many adoptions. It suggests that, at least in some cases, abortion may be a better solution to an unwanted pregnancy than giving up the child for adoption.[57]

---

56. Laurino, "Unwanted Infant," 37.

57. For further reading, see: Eldridge, *Twenty Things*; Guida-Richards, *What White Parents*; MacFarquhar, "The Fog."

Laurino thus highlights how politics has clouded the abortion issue:

> Adoption is the new front line in the ongoing battle for women's bodily autonomy, and the anti-abortion movement is using adopted children as its political football. The only moral solution to an unwanted pregnancy, this thinking asserts, is for women to do the right thing: carry the baby to term and relinquish the child for adoption.[58]

CONCLUSION

Evangelical Christians and the Roman Catholic Church teach that abortion is sinful because life begins at conception, but there are other positions. In fact, several Christian churches have issued formal statements affirming a woman's right to choose abortion in at least some circumstances. The Evangelical Lutheran Church in America not only permits abortion but labels it a "responsible choice" or at least "permissible" in several circumstances. Similarly, the Episcopal Church states its respect for the mother's individual conscience. The Presbyterian Church USA states that a woman's decision to abort can be "morally acceptable" in "problem pregnancies." These official church positions are directly contrary to the Catholic position that abortion is "gravely contrary to the moral law" and to the Southern Baptist position that abortion is equivalent to "genocide." The fact that Christian churches are not absolutely in sync on this matter perhaps reflects the seriousness of the decision to abort.

McGlasson argues that the focus on abortion has gotten out of hand. The churches and religious people should remember that Jesus would want great concern for women who become pregnant and for all children, poor as well as middle-class. Also, churches need to be concerned about such critical issues as the environment, the death penalty, poverty, social justice, and healthcare. Note that the Catholic Church has spoken out against capital punishment in a consistent right to life ethic. So McGlasson is not advocating for abortion but he argues that it is only one moral issue among many and that the right to life focus has ignored these other critical issues.

Collins focuses on the question of Biblical values. His direct conclusion is that Bible does not affirm the morality or immorality of abortion. Collins states that the Bible simply does not address abortion as an ethical

---

58. Laurino, "Unwanted Infant," 36.

issue. Thus for those trying to discern What Would Jesus Do?, there is no clear answer.

Peters argues that the right to life position is flawed theologically and in its entire characterization. She argues that women are not simply childbearers and mothers, forever subservient to men. Rather than posit that personhood begins at conception, she sees that becoming a human is a process and the focus of the abortion debate should see women as trying to make moral choices about an unwanted pregnancy.

Kamitsuka presents a scholarly treatise that logically disputes the pro-life philosophical, scientific, and theological position that the fetus is a human person from the moment of conception. She painstakingly demonstrates that both Old Testament and New Testament arguments in favor of fetal personhood do not stand scholarly scrutiny. She also criticizes the pro-life argument that the parable of the Good Samaritan teaches that women have a duty to birth the child and then care for it, disputes claims of biblical authority against abortion, and offers a theologically grounded ethical case for a woman's right to choose abortion in many circumstances. She concludes that the fetus does have value but the mother has the right to make the abortion decision.

Dworkin, a law professor, makes a provocative case that the abortion debate is flawed. The usual framing of the debate as a right to life for the fetus because the fetus is a human person versus respect for the woman's right to choose is erroneous, says Dworkin. He argues that both sides actually agree that human life is sacred. What is lost in the usual debate, however, is the recognition that there are two aspects of respect for the sanctity of life. One is biological; cells are alive. The second is one's investment in life. Every one of us humans invests time, effort, and work into, hopefully, a life well lived.

Bioethicists Gutman and Moreno state that a key contention is the question of when a fetus becomes a human person. They contend that this debate is "impossible" and "is not resolvable by reason alone."[59] The pro-life position that the fetus is a human person means that traditional Christians have tremendous difficulty in accepting any softening in their position. As noted above, there are scholars such as Kaczor[60] who offer strong defenses of the pro-life position. Readers are advised to consult such scholars to make a well-informed decision on this issue.

59. Gutman and Moreno, *Everybody Wants*, 61.
60. Kaczor, *The Ethics of Abortion*.

As with the rest of this book, the objective is not to argue that one of these positions is the correct position. The objective is to demonstrate that while many preachers—and often churches such as the Catholic Church and the Southern Baptist Convention—sincerely believe that there is one and only one position, there are other Christian churches and conscientious scholars who can and do take other positions. And they back those positions up with biblical and theological scholarship, historical research, logical argumentation, philosophical-ethical arguments, and even common sense reasoning. Furthermore, on this issue at least three churches—the Episcopal Church, the Evangelical Lutheran Church in America, the Presbyterian Church USA—make some allowance for abortion.

The fact that 62 percent of all Americans—and similar percentages of white, nonevangelical Protestants, Catholics, and Black Protestants—say that abortion should be legal in all or most cases, makes clear that churches proclaiming a rigid pro-life message are not meeting with full acceptance. Those churches can continue to condemn abortion or they can look at churches such as the Evangelical Lutheran Church in America that offer a more nuanced position. Positions on abortion seem too rigid to hope for much, if any, movement. Despite her strong pro-choice treatise, Kamisutka observes, "Since Christianity is a historically expansive and diversely lived tradition, the abortion question can never be answered definitively for all Christians."[61]

One point that perhaps churches can agree on is McGlasson's reminder that abortion is only one moral issue. The focus on abortion in the last twenty years has often resulted in considerable neglect of other issues. Another point to consider is that adoption is not an easy and complete alternative to abortion. Despite the best of intentions, adoptive parents cannot completely prevent their adopted children from feeling at some point in their lives the pain of feeling "rejected" by their birth mothers and cross-racial adoptions face the difficulty of parents being able to help their adopted children reach clear racial identity.

---

61. Kamitsuka, *Abortion*, 3.

CHAPTER 8

Physician-Assisted Suicide

"The breath of life in all human beings is a gift from God (Genesis 2:7) and thus inherently holy." —(National Association of Evangelicals)

"In short, a God not totally obsessed with the sheer quantity of our lives may well have purposes for us that are incompatible with longer life—even if we want to live longer." —John Hardwig

"The history of the law's treatment of assisted suicide in this country has been and continues to be one of the rejection of nearly all efforts to permit it."
—Chief Justice Rehnquist in *Washington et al. v. Glucksberg et al.* (1997)

INTRODUCTION

LIKE ABORTION, EUTHANASIA IS a life and death issue, making it one of the most difficult decisions in life. Many churchgoers are likely to hear that physician-assisted suicide is immoral and sinful. Catholics, for example, claim to be pro-life across the board—thus opposed to abortion, euthanasia, and the death penalty. The Catechism of the Catholic Church states that euthanasia is "morally unacceptable" and "forbidden."[1] Similarly, the Southern Baptist Convention has issued a Resolution affirming "the biblical prohibition against the taking of innocent human life by another person,

1. USCCB, CCC, 2277

or oneself, through euthanasia or assisted suicide."[2] Specifically, the SBC "rejects as appropriate any action which, of itself or by intention, causes a person's death."[3] Contrary to its pro-choice position on abortion, the Evangelical Lutheran Church in America notes that patients have a right to refuse treatment but does not go so far as to permit physician-assisted suicide:

> We oppose the legalization of physician-assisted death, which would allow the private killing of one person by another. Public control and regulation of such actions would be extremely difficult, if not impossible. The potential for abuse, especially of people who are most vulnerable, would be substantially increased.
>
> Caring treatment that allows death to occur within the bounds of what is morally acceptable may help reduce the appeal of physician-assisted death. Hospice care offers promise of more humane treatment at the end of life. A more equitable health care system that more effectively responds to catastrophic illness and provides the needed follow-up care should also be a priority for those concerned about end-of-life decisions.[4]

Finally, the National Association of Evangelicals recognizes the intent of ethical persons to alleviate suffering but still leaves no room for euthanasia:

> As evangelicals, we deny that there are any circumstances that justify euthanasia; that is, intentionally ending a life through medical intervention. One should be wary of the many euphemisms for assisted suicide such as "physician-assisted death," "aid in dying," "death with dignity," and the like.[5]

Once again opinion polls show that many Americans disagree. In fact, a majority of Americans say that doctor-assisted suicide is morally acceptable. Specifically, in 2022 55 percent of Americans said it is morally acceptable while 41 percent said it is morally wrong.[6] So a majority of Americans say physician-assisted suicide is morally acceptable despite major denominations saying that it is immoral.

---

2. Southern Baptist Convention, "Resolution on Euthanasia."
3. Southern Baptist Convention, "Resolution on Euthanasia."
4. Evangelical Lutheran Church in America, "End of Life Decisions," 4.
5. National Association of Evangelicals (NAE), *Allowing Natural Death*.
6. Brenan, "Americans Say."

From these church statements, it is clear that many Christian churches regard physician-assisted suicide as contrary to God's law. They see God as the Author of life and only He determines when each of us dies. We are not permitted to take our own lives and assisting one in suicide is tantamount to murder.

In living, however, situations arise that confront all of us with the complexity of the decision to leave the question of the time of death to God or to take action to hasten death. We ourselves or a loved one are diagnosed with a fatal disease. Or a horrible accident leaves one in a hopeless situation where living is reduced to surviving on a ventilator. Or the "blessing" of a long life becomes the curse of suffering from Alzheimer's and knowing that one's cognitive faculties will slowly disintegrate. In light of such circumstances, some writers have explored other answers to the question of assisted suicide.

HARDWIG: A DUTY TO DIE

Philosophy professor John Hardwig goes further than saying euthanasia is ethical; he asserts that there can be a duty to die.[7] He gives the hypothetical example of a senior citizen who is diagnosed with a serious or terminal illness. The doctor informs the senior that he/she can fight the disease and perhaps live an extra year or two but it will be costly and it will mean that his/her adult children will need to give him/her considerable care during treatment. So trying to prolong life may cost the person's children money (a smaller inheritance and perhaps lost salary due to caring for the parent) and time and effort. If the person declines fighting the illness, he or she can help his/her adult children (and perhaps grandchildren) considerably.

Hardwig argues that the person may, therefore, have a duty to die—a duty to refrain from prolonging his or her life. He even goes so far as to advocate suicide: family-assisted suicide or physician-assisted suicide, preferably the latter. He notes that doctors' extensive knowledge of both drugs and dying makes them well qualified to assist a person who wants to die. While family-assisted suicide may be apt at times, more often physician-assisted suicide is the better course of action. For one, there is "very little legal risk in a physician-assisted suicide, especially if the family is in agreement."[8] Hardwig also notes that suicide is not as easy as it seems. Quite a few people

---

7. Hardwig, "Dying at the Right Time," 81–100.
8. Hardwig, "Dying at the Right Time," 95.

botch suicide attempts and end up with serious issues such as a partially blown off face from a gunshot that did not kill them.

Hardwig notes that many religious people oppose suicide because they believe that God alone decides when we are supposed to die. In response, he notes that human efforts to prolong life (e .g., medical interventions) might be thwarting God's intended time for our death. So if humans can prolong life beyond God's intended date, why is it wrong to shorten life ahead of God's intended date? Second, he suggests that perhaps God wants us humans to step up to the plate, so to speak, and bring about our own death or the death of a relative: "God may want me to step up and assume the responsibility for ending my own life or for seeing that someone else's suffering is ended."[9]

This argument is parallel to the believer who complained to God that God did not intervene to save him in a crisis when he passed up several offers of help and God says that those offers were His acts of divine intervention! Hardwig suggests that religious believers should consider the possibility of the existence of "a God not totally obsessed with the sheer quantity of our lives."[10]

Part of Hardwig's rationale parallels Dworkin's argument (see below) that respect for the sanctity of life includes not only the biological aspect of life but also what one does with or invests in his or her life. To repeat, all of us strive to make something of our lives and therefore put time and energy into getting an education, starting and finishing a career, entering relationships especially marriage, and raising a family. All of us seek a life well lived. In David Brooks' terms, we seek a vocation and what he calls "eulogy virtues": "They're the virtues that get talked about at your funeral, the ones that exist at the core of your being—whether you are kind, brave, honest or faithful; what kind of relationships you formed."[11]

Hardwig argues that if one is older, e.g., seventy or eighty years old and has had the good fortune to have lived a good life—college degree, career, marriage and family or however one defines a "good life"—then he or she, facing the option to prolong life but at the cost of one's adult child/children having to expend considerable time and effort and perhaps money, should choose to put their child or children ahead of their desire to live a year or two longer. Whoever who has been fortunate enough to live

---

9. Hardwig, "Dying at the Right Time," 86.
10. Hardwig, "Dying at the Right Time," 85.
11. Brooks, *The Road to Character*, xi.

seven or more decades and has been fortunate to make something of his or her life, should not ask an adult child to sacrifice to gain an additional year or two. Dworkin would say that such a decision to not ask a child to prolong the life of a person with much of life's experience successfully navigated shows sincere respect for life—respect for the life of one's adult child. It allows one's child to keep investing in his/her life, to make his/her life as meaningful as possible.

THE CATHOLIC POSITION

Although the Catechism of the Catholic Church states that euthanasia is "morally unacceptable" and "forbidden," the Catholic Church does allow choosing to forego certain medical treatments that would prolong life. Catholic teaching posits that believers can refuse medical procedures that are "burdensome, dangerous, extraordinary, or disproportionate to the expected outcome."[12]

It is also critical to note that Catholic teaching is aware that administering certain painkillers can lead to death, but that giving these drugs is not forbidden:

> The use of painkillers to alleviate the sufferings of the dying, even at the risk of shortening their days, can be morally in conformity with human dignity if death is not willed as either an end or a means, but only foreseen and tolerated as inevitable. Palliative care is a special form of disinterested charity. As such it should be encouraged.[13]

In one of their Directives for Catholic health care services, the United States Bishops reiterate that pain medications are permissible "so long as the intent is not to hasten death."[14] They go on to note the redemptive value of suffering and the importance of allowing the patient sufficient consciousness to prepare for death.

This position that painkillers can be used even if they cause eventual death follows St. Thomas Aquinas' *Summa Theologica*. Specifically, it is the principle of double effect wherein a second unintended effect is ethical if there is an ethical intended primary effect. Bioethicists Gutman and

12. USCCB, CCC, 2277.
13. USCCB, CCC, 2277.
14. USCCB, "Ethical And Religious Directives," Directive 61.

Moreno note that this use of painkillers which cause death can be very similar to a doctor such as Jack Kevorkian administering drugs that directly cause death.[15] The only difference is the time factor. An act by a doctor like Kevorkian causes immediate death; administration of barbiturates causes death, just more slowly.

Parenthetically, the principle of double effect has also been used to justify such acts as the dropping of the atomic bombs on Hiroshima and Nagasaki. The primary intent was to end the war; the secondary effect was the death of hundreds of thousands of Japanese citizens.

One note: theologians or philosophers who cite the double effect argument obviously are going beyond Scripture, beyond what Jesus would say! This is a clear example of the difference between Catholic theologians and philosophers and many Protestant scholars. Protestants rely heavily on the Bible and are less inclined to rely on philosophical arguments such as St. Thomas's focus on the principle of double effect.

"Extraordinary" often boils down to rather "ordinary" treatments. In other words, Catholics can refrain from even rather ordinary medical interventions with no guilt. A Catholic does not have to have open heart surgery or undergo chemotherapy if she chooses not to, with no reprimands from the Catholic Church.

Thus Catholics cannot seek physician-assisted suicide but they can use pain medications that may lead to death and they do not have to use every possible medical option to stay alive.

COLLINS ON THE BIBLE AND EUTHANASIA

Biblical scholar Collins does not explicitly address euthanasia but it appears that his comments on abortion are apropos. Namely, the Bible does not directly address the issue.[16] At the time of Jesus, life expectancy was not that long, compared to twenty-first century America. Second, medicine and healthcare were not that advanced. If you contracted many diseases, you would die rather quickly. Jesus brought Lazarus back from the dead but did not have to deal with anyone suffering unbearable pain from Lou Gehrig's disease or the devastating effects of Alzheimer's.

---

15. Gutman and Moreno, "Everybody Wants."
16. Collins, *What Are Biblical Values?*

THE SUICIDE TOURIST

A PBS documentary, *The Suicide Tourist*, portrayed how this issue affected one man suffering from ALS, also known as Lou Gehrig's disease. Craig Ewert was a college professor who decided to move to England with his wife after their two children were grown. It was an early retirement move, and they planned to spend the rest of their lives in Great Britain. Sadly, Craig was diagnosed with ALS. The documentary begins with the disease having progressed considerably. Craig is now confined to a wheelchair and also needs oxygen to help with his breathing. His wife has become his nurse who feeds him and cares for him everyday. Craig thinks that his death is imminent. Craig has learned that Switzerland allows persons facing death to come in and avail themselves of physician-assisted suicide. There is an organization that advises such persons how to commit suicide. The person does have to be capable of administering the lethal potion to himself/herself.

Ewert notes that he is an atheist so he is not constrained by any religious dictates. He argues that he is going to die very soon either way, "naturally" or via suicide in Switzerland. He argues that trying to live as long as possible naturally would just mean more pain and suffering for him and his wife, so he chooses suicide tourism in Switzerland.

Similar to this scenario, the (in)famous Dr. Jack Kevorkian killed a patient, Thomas Youk, suffering from ALS (Lou Gehrig's Disease) and went to prison for it. Youk had fought ALS for years and was having difficulty breathing. He sought out Kevorkian to end his pain and suffering because he feared that very soon he was going to choke to death. CBS (60 Minutes) reported on Kevorkian's action and on reactions to those actions.

So both the 60 Minutes reporting on Dr. Kevorkian and the PBS documentary show ALS patients where the disease has progressed to the point that they are most likely very close to death. Kevorkian actually killing Youk and Craig Ewert killing himself in Switzerland (with the aid of a society dedicated to such suicides) involve two individuals who have fought Lou Gehrig's disease for quite some time and are now almost 100% incapacitated and want to end their lives before ALS most likely suffocates them to death.

Utilitarian philosophers decide ethical issues by weighing the positive and negative consequences of an action.[17] Here physician-assisted suicide

---

17. See, e.g., Souryal and Whitehead, *Ethics in Criminal Justice*.

alleviates pain and suffering both for the patient and for any caregiver such as Craig Ewert's wife. Suicide would also end the medical expenses both men and their families were facing.

As noted above, the religious argument against such suicide is that God is the Author of life and only He decides when we are to die (recall Hardwig's comments on this issue above). Christianity also argues that suffering is salvific, that our human suffering can be a sharing in the redemptive suffering of Jesus.

Although official church teaching, such as that of the Catholic Church, points to God's will about when life ends and about the positive value of suffering, on a human level it seems hard to defend. Thomas Youk, Kevorkian's patient, was paralyzed and lying in bed all day. He was becoming terrified that ALS was going to cause him to suffocate to death, and afraid of the pain of such a death. Ewert appears a bit more detached but he simply does not see much value in prolonging a life that is becoming less and less any sort of active life and which is going to be more and more painful. He is also concerned about his wife having to do more and more just to help him get through a few more days of around the clock nursing care.

THE PRO-LIFE RESPONSE TO *THE SUICIDE TOURIST*

Fr. Tad Pacholczyk, Director of Education for the National Catholic Bioethics Center, has written a response to the argument that ALS or other terminal illness patients can say that their quality of life has become so low that they feel life is not worth living. Fr. Pacholczyk cites the late ALS patient John Peyton who, like Craig Ewert suffered from ALS to the point he was totally dependent on friends and family. Despite his terrible suffering, John argued that his loving support made his life worthwhile: "I have loving support all around me. I don't understand how anyone could deny that I have a very high quality of life, and it gets me to understand and be compassionate toward those without the support that I have."[18]

THE DUTCH EXPERIENCE

According to a recent study, 4.7 percent of the deaths in Holland now are the result of physician-assisted suicide, up from 1.7 percent prior to the

---

18. Pacholczyk, "The 'Quality of Life' Error."

legalization of the practice in 2002. In 2015 about 8 percent of those who died asked for help but help was only provided in about half of those requests.[19] The lesson appears to be that if physician-assisted suicide is made legal, the numbers will go up. It is now legal in several states in the United States.

Some people, including Dutch doctors, are concerned that the Dutch law has gone too far. One issue is patients asserting their autonomy over their doctor's concerns that the patient may still have months or even years of life left. The patient may think that the pain is too much but the doctor may think that it is tolerable. For example, one woman cancelled her physiotherapy that would have alleviated her condition and made her condition seem critical.[20] In short, legislators may enact a law that tries to limit the numbers of physician–assisted suicides to extreme cases but citizens may seek physician-assisted suicide for reasons not necessarily congruent with the intent of the lawmakers. On the other hand, if physician-assisted suicide is not available, a spouse may go out shopping and come home to see either a successful or a botched suicide.

Ethics professor Theo Boer, a former supporter of euthanasia, now thinks that the practice has gone too far in the Netherlands. First, he thinks that the numbers have increased as more and more people seek physician-assisted suicide. Second, he disagrees with some of the reasons for requesting it. He notes, for example, that in his review of five hundred recent cases, fifty individuals listed loneliness as their reason for requesting physician-assisted suicide. Another development is when a caregiver develops terminal cancer and the patient that was being tended for seeks to die on the same day that the caregiver dies.[21]

DWORKIN'S ARGUMENT

Ronald M. Dworkin, a deceased law professor, uses the same reasoning about euthanasia that he uses with abortion (see Chapter 7). He contends that respect for the sanctity of life involves both the biological fact of life and one's investment in life.[22] Consider Craig Ewert. Dworkin would argue Ewert has lived a successful life. He has had what appears to be a loving

19. CBS News, "Euthanasia Deaths."
20. deBellaigue, "Death on Demand."
21. Boer, "Dutch Experiences," 25–26.
22. Dworkin, *Life's Dominion*.

marriage, he and his wife have raised two children who are now independent adults, and both he and his wife have been successful professionally. They even started to have an enviable retirement, taking early retirement to move to Great Britain, a destination they both wanted. But ALS is ending their idyllic retirement.

Dworkin would argue that ALS has forestalled Craig from making any further investment in life. The disease has also put his wife into the role of her husband's nurse. While she appears to have accepted this role, it has prevented her from doing other things professionally with her life. So Dworkin would say that both Ewerts have respected life; they have invested themselves in marriage, family, and careers. ALS, not Ewert, shows lack of respect for the sanctity of life because the disease has made Craig unable to keep investing in life, to persist in making a meaningful life. Euthanasia is simply hastening Craig's demise by a few days (months at most) and it would allow his wife to return to making investments in her own life. This is not meant to diminish her role as nurse to her husband. Clearly, she loved her husband so much that she has taken care of him in his fight with ALS for some period of time.

In Dworkin's own words:

> People who want an early, peaceful death for themselves or their relatives are not rejecting or denigrating the sanctity of life; on the contrary, they believe that a quicker death shows more respect for life than a protracted one. Once again, both sides in the debate about euthanasia share a concern for life's sanctity; they are united by that value, and disagree only about how best to interpret and respect it."[23]

Parenthetically, writer David Brooks makes the same point when he notes that at funerals speakers note the deceased person's "eulogy virtues;" they praise people for the character they displayed in life, for the sense of vocation that their lives embodied, not simply for how long they lived.[24]

---

23. Dworkin, *Life's Dominion*, 238.
24. Brooks, *The Road to Character*.

ANOTHER DWORKIN'S VIEW

In *Artificial Happiness*,[25] anesthesiologist Ronald W. Dworkin warns that the current ethos of both doctors and patients may well lead to a substantial increase in physician-assisted suicides in the near future. His main contention is that primary care doctors have been overprescribing drugs like Zoloft for some time as they have "discovered" a "new" disease, unhappiness. The fact that such drugs can affect the neurotransmitters and thereby dull feelings of unhappiness and depression has led doctors to overprescribe them and patients to demand them. The problem, according to Dworkin, is that because these drugs make patients feel better they also reduce or eliminate any incentive to address whatever problem is causing the unhappiness or depression. So the patient experiences happiness, not due to solving the cause of one's unhappiness or sadness, but because the pill dulls the pain, hence the term "artificial happiness."

As for end of life issues, Dworkin contends that the logical progression of the use of these drugs is to see old age and impending death as just one more place for doctors to intervene and end any pain or suffering. After a doctor and patient have resorted to such drugs to stop life problems at middle age, both will be ready for the doctor to end any pain, depression, or unhappiness at age sixty-five or older. So Dworkin sees a sizable increase in the number of physician-assisted suicides in the near future.

THE HUMAN/HUMANE ARGUMENT

Christian churches speak of a loving and compassionate God (in accordance with the Gospels and Epistles of John). It is difficult to believe that such a loving God wants His children to undergo maximum suffering. Both Thomas Youk and Craig Ewert had already suffered considerably. Both had had ALS for some time and were then paralyzed and experiencing difficulty breathing. It is not the case that these men were diagnosed with ALS while still healthy and immediately chose to commit suicide months or years before the disease would kill them. Both were apparently close to death, perhaps only a day or few days or at most weeks away from death.

Even if you believe in the value of suffering, these men had suffered considerably. Physician-assisted suicide would simply avert a day or two or a few days or months of final suffering. It is hard to imagine that an

---

25. Dworkin, *Artificial Happiness*.

all-loving deity wants us to endure every last minute of physical suffering because He alone is the author of life, or, in Hardwig's words, to think of God as someone totally obsessed with the sheer quantity of our lives. It seems more loving, more compassionate to envision a God who allows us to end life a day or week or perhaps a few months early because we are in unbearable pain. Furthermore, that pain necessarily involves loved ones. Both of these men had loving wives who were caring for them and who had to watch their husbands suffer day after day.

As noted above, Fr. Pacholczyk makes the argument that ALS sufferers can imitate patient John Peyton who felt that his wonderful support system of friends and family gave him a "marvelous" quality of life.[26] While one can admire Peyton's courageous outlook, one can also question whether all such terminal patients can or should be forced to endure extreme pain and suffering. Not all of us are equipped to be as strong as John Peyton was.

One could argue that if God demands such unmitigated suffering, He appears to be a sadist, or at least a partial sadist. Religions such as the Catholic Church and the SBC that condemn euthanasia have no problem with modern medicine and surgery. It is perfectly acceptable to use drugs or have surgery to deal with an injury or illness that produces pain. But if a patient is at the end of his or her life and seeks to end it a bit early, that action is condemned as immoral and sinful.

Opponents also argue the slippery slope argument that legalizing euthanasia will open the floodgates. Today it might be limited to true end of life situations such as ALS patients months or years in disease progression. Tomorrow advocates might argue that elderly individuals are experiencing diminished quality of life and they should be allowed to end their lives if they so choose.

A response is that laws can be crafted to limit euthanasia to the terminally ill. And laws could spell out that simply suffering old age is not a qualifier. Similarly, laws could prohibit euthanasia for those suffering from depression. More positively, efforts can be made to alleviate the loneliness that many seniors experience which can lead to depression. To favor euthanasia does not mean that one wants to kill off hordes of elderly citizens or hordes of nursing home patients. Laws can be crafted to limit euthanasia to severe cases where individuals are close to dying from horrible and painful diseases such as ALS and where it is compassionate to afford them that option.

26. Pacholczyk, "The 'Quality of Life' Error."

A troubling issue is Alzheimer's disease. Anyone who has had a relative suffer this disease knows its heartbreak. My mother-in-law suffered the disease for about four years, with her last years in a nursing home. Early on, she lost her memory. She did not recognize her husband of decades or her only child, her daughter, my wife.

Unlike ALS, Alzheimer's patients do not appear to suffer physically. The horror of the disease is that they lose their minds. In a very real sense, they are dead; their minds have, for all intents and purposes, died.

In Dworkin's terms, they are no longer capable of investing in their lives. And all the investing that they made in their lives, their years of building a career, starting and persisting in a loving marriage, and perhaps raising children, is now closed off forever. So following Dworkin's argument that the sanctity of life includes this dimension of investing in one's life, one could argue that ending a biological life does not show disrespect for the other aspect of respect for life.

Someone suffering from ALS, inoperable cancer, or a similar situation makes a strong case for physician-assisted suicide. If a person is literally only days, weeks, or even months away from a "natural" death, hastening death but a short time seems preferable to mandating that the patient suffer every last day of pain. The case of Alzheimer's disease may be more controversial but at least in Dworkin's view, it too presents a case for allowing physician-assisted suicide.

COMPARISON

If one follows traditional teaching such as that of the Catholic Church and the Southern Baptist Convention, the positive side is that this view clearly respects the sanctity of life. Traditional teaching respects life to its natural end. Many believers also feel that their suffering shares in the redemptive suffering of Christ. The negative side of this teaching is that some terminally ill or otherwise afflicted patients may suffer when euthanasia would end the suffering. They may suffer unbearable physical pain and/or they may suffer the psychological pain of simply being alive, of thinking that they are breathing but not living what Dworkin would consider a meaningful life. In Hardwig's terms, they very well could think that they are beyond their past-due date, that they have lived beyond what would have been a more logical end to their lives. The extreme example of living beyond a meaningful life is that point in the life of an Alzheimer's patient when he or

PHYSICIAN-ASSISTED SUICIDE

she no longer has any idea who he/she is or who one's spouse and children are. Another negative aspect is that denial of physician-assisted suicide can lead some to try suicide on their own or with the help of relatives or friends. Those attempts can fail or cause a number of serious consequences due to inappropriate doses of medications and so on.

Another negative side of traditional teaching is that it can lead some terminally ill patients to forego food and/or water in an attempt to bring on death. A problem with this is that avoiding food and hydration can be a slow, painful death. Accordingly, ethicist James Rachels argues that "sometimes it is better to actively kill a person than to let him die in a slow process that produces more suffering than actually killing him would."[27]

A final negative aspect of adhering to the strict pro-life position of the Catholic Church and other churches is that it leads to religious leaders or scholars turning to arguments such as St. Thomas' principle of double effect. It leads religious individuals to engage in what looks like mental gymnastics to justify their actions. If they want to justify ending the pain of a terminally ill patient, they argue that they are just giving the person enough drugs to kill the pain. They are fully aware that these painkillers can and will end life. But they then point to the principle of double effect as a cover. "We never intended death directly. We wanted to end the pain and suffering. It just so happens that ending the person's pain also ended their life!" This is analogous to the case of divorce (see Chapter 6) where the Catholic Church mitigates a strict no-divorce policy by approving more applications for annulment. As noted in that chapter, this can mean that a man who was married for years and has children is granted an annulment saying the marriage is null and void—it never happened! One can argue that a more honest approach in both cases is to simply say 1) physician-assisted death is ethical and 2) divorce is ethical. Jesus did not seem to be the type of leader who sought covers. It seems that He spoke directly and that He would be more comfortable with church leaders who did the same.

The positive consequences of physician-assisted suicide are that it can eliminate unbearable pain and that it can end one's life when one wants, when an individual feels that he or she is no longer living a meaningful life but is simply existing. It can also serve to end the life of one who has a disease such as Alzheimer's or ALS and who does not want to lose their mind (Alzheimer's) or lose complete control of their physical functions (ALS). And, as just noted, it is a more "honest" approach compared to

---

27. Quoted in Fiala, *What Would Jesus*, 86.

relying on the principle of double effect to allow one to think that he or she is ethical when in fact he/she is clearly intending the death of the patient. The negative side of viewpoints such as those of law professor Dworkin and philosopher Hardwig is that the practice and the endorsement of physician-assisted suicide can lead to less respect for life and possibly to the situation where people choose death when they could still have meaningful months or even years ahead of them. Some persons may choose physician-assisted suicide when pain medication could possibly alleviate all or most or much of their pain. And perhaps they could accomplish one or more achievements that could very possibly help a number of other people. Finally, if physician-assisted suicide were to become commonplace, it is possible that persons suffering dementia would become candidates very early after their diagnosis of dementia.

CONCLUSION

As with abortion, the Catholic Church and the Southern Baptist Convention and other Christian churches condemn euthanasia. They see God as the author of life and argue that God, not any of us, can choose when we are to die. So preachers in those denominations normally preach that physician-assisted suicide is wrong. The Evangelical Lutheran Church in America also declares physician-assisted suicide wrong, whereas on abortion it took a position allowing abortion in several circumstances. The Bible forbids murder but does not explicitly address physician-assisted suicide as it was not an issue for biblical authors. Polls, however, show that a majority of Americans see euthanasia as morally acceptable. Also, there are scholars such as Hardwig and Dworkin who present reasonable arguments permitting euthanasia. Philosopher Hardwig presents an intriguing argument that there may be a duty to die. Law professor Dworkin argues that respect for life includes trying to make one's life meaningful and that either terminal illness or a sickness such as Alzheimer's can mean that living is no longer meaningful. Doctor Ronald Dworkin, on the other hand, contends that the rise of drugs such as Zoloft to treat unhappiness will most likely lead to increased instances of physician-assisted suicide in the future as the next step in doctors' efforts to promote artificial happiness.

Apart from the scholarly debate, a documentary such as *The Suicide Tourist* makes a compelling case for physician-assisted suicide. Watching a person such as Craig Ewert—once a productive college professor, a loving husband, and a caring father—suffer the devastation of ALS is heartbreaking. Ewert has gone from what he was, a person who chose to retire early and live in England with his wife, to an invalid who relies on his wife to be his constant nurse. And the disease has progressed so far that death is only days, weeks, or at most a couple of months away. The choice is that one believes that suffering more than Ewert already has is God's will or that God does not have a problem with a person choosing to avoid even more suffering and also spare one's life partner from going through that suffering as well.

A final word: If the Catholic Church and the Southern Baptist Convention are correct that physician-assisted suicide is immoral, it seems reasonable to think that an all-loving God would have mercy on a person suffering from a terminal illness such as ALS or a horrible cancer who opted to seek an early death. The Jesus of the Gospels had harsh words for hypocrites but compassion for the sick and infirm. Surely a God who knows our innermost heart and thoughts would understand the suffering that drove both Thomas Youk and Craig Ewert to seek death rather than further suffering.

The experience of the Netherlands shows that there can be problems with legalizing physician-assisted suicide. It appears that the numbers have increased there and that some people are seeking death when they become lonely or depressed. Failure to legalize euthanasia would prevent such problems but failure to legalize the practice could mean that persons suffering what they consider unbearable pain and suffering might resort to suicide, to simply killing themselves or trying to kill themselves (failed attempts).

So there are positions contrary to what many preachers and churches say is clearcut religious doctrine. However, as noted, we leave it to each reader to judge for him/herself whether traditional teaching or a particular theologian or scholar is correct. And in this matter of physician-assisted suicide, it also appears that neither side of the debate is problem free. Both allowing and prohibiting the practice have positive and negative consequences.

Finally, since this is such a critical issue, readers are advised to consult scholars who argue against physician-assisted suicide. Issues as serious as this deserve full consideration before deciding which course of action is best.

CHAPTER 9

The Death Penalty

"Capital punishment offers no justice to victims, but rather encourages revenge."—Pope Francis

"You can't reconcile being pro-life on abortion and pro-death on the death penalty."—N. T. Wright

"Why do we want to kill all the broken people? What is wrong with us, that we think a thing like that can be right?"—Bryan Stevenson, *Just Mercy, A Story of Justice and Redemption*

INTRODUCTION

ONE MIGHT THINK THAT the death penalty is a straightforward issue: Should a heinous murderer be executed or not for deliberately killing someone in a gruesome manner? One might think that Christians would agree on what Jesus would want them to do about capital punishment. One might assume that God would give Christians a clear indication of what He thinks about such an issue. After all, this is a critical issue. If God favors the death penalty, that means His followers should take the life of the murderer. If God opposes the death penalty, then believers should oppose the death penalty and the murderer should be allowed to live.

The choices seem very clear. So it might seem reasonable to think that churches would agree on one clear choice. Well, not that simple. Catholics argue that Christian teaching is completely opposed to the death penalty. Southern Baptists argue that God has ordained capital punishment for first degree murderers. So two of the biggest and most influential Christian denominations are diametrically opposed in their interpretation of what God wants! So as far as the death penalty is concerned, Catholic churchgoers are likely to hear sermons and read official church statements against the death penalty. Southern Baptists, on the other hand, are likely to hear preaching and read Southern Baptist Convention official resolutions in favor of the death penalty. A Frontline documentary on Sister Helen Prejean, for example, features a police officer who arrested one of the murderers that Sister Prejean counseled in prison. He cites his church's pro-death penalty stance as part of his rationale for being pro–death penalty.

THE TEACHING OF SEVERAL CHURCHES

Pope Francis[1] and the U.S. Catholic Bishops[2] have both issued formal statements opposing the death penalty. The Catechism of the Catholic Church was amended in 2016 to read as follows: "Consequently, the Church teaches, in the light of the Gospel, that the death penalty is inadmissible because it is an attack on the inviolability and dignity of the person, and she works with determination for its abolition worldwide."[3] In 2024 the Vatican reaffirmed that the death penalty is a grave violation of human dignity.[4]

The Southern Baptist Convention, on the other hand, has formally endorsed capital punishment as ordained by God. The SBC relies on several Old Testament references and the Letter of Paul to the Romans as evidence that God favors the death penalty (details below).[5]

The Lutheran Church-Missouri Synod echoes the pro-death penalty position of the Southern Baptist Convention, including citing Old Testament verses and Romans 13 as Scriptural support. However, it also offers a caveat: the government does not have to utilize capital punishment "if it determines that some other form of punishment would better serve society at large at a particular time and place."[6]

1. Pope Francis, *Encyclical Fratelli Tutti (All Brothers)*.
2. USCCB, "Statement on Capital Punishment."
3. USCCB, CCC, 2267.
4. Dicastery for the Doctrine of the Faith, *Human Dignity*.
5. Southern Baptist Convention, "Resolution on Capital Punishment."
6. Lutheran Church-Missouri Synod. "FAQS: Death Penalty."

It is interesting to compare the Biblical sources of the Catholic Church and Southern Baptist Convention. The Catholic Bishops mention several teachings of Jesus, including forgiveness of injuries (Matt 18:21–35), reconciliation with those who have injured us (Matt 5:43–45), and praying for forgiveness as we have forgiven others (Matt 6:12).[7] The Bishops reaffirmed their opposition to the death penalty in 2000. The Southern Baptist resolution, on the other hand, offers no specific teaching of Jesus in support of its position. Instead it offers Old Testament (Hebrew Bible) verses and St. Paul's Letter to the Romans (Chapter 13) which forbids personal revenge but allegedly authorizes the civil authority to punish those guilty of capital murder.[8]

The Presbyterian Church USA opposes the death penalty. In 1959 the 171st General Assembly, "believing that capital punishment cannot be condoned by an interpretation of the Bible based upon the revelation of God's love in Jesus Christ," called on Christians to "seek the redemption of evil doers and not their death" and noted that "the use of the death penalty tends to brutalize the society that condones it."[9] In 2000, and a decade later in 2010, the General Assembly reaffirmed its stance against capital punishment, and called for "an immediate moratorium on all executions in all jurisdictions that impose capital punishment," authorizing direct advocacy by the Stated Clerk with the President of the United States, Congressional representatives, and governors and state legislators in states where persons are executed.[10]

CRIMINOLOGISTS

Before examining what theology professors say about this issue, we first offer scholarly opinions from criminologists. We do this because many believers support their faith position with claims that the death penalty deters potential murderers or that the death penalty is more economical than a life sentence. Many legislators also endorse the argument that the death penalty deters as a supposedly proven and irrefutable fact.

Criminologists have researched capital punishment extensively and offer important insights about it. First, extensive research has raised serious

---

7. United States Catholic Bishops, "Statement on Capital Punishment."
8. SBC, "Resolution on Capital Punishment."
9. Presbyterian Church USA, "What We Believe."
10. Presbyterian Church USA, "What We Believe."

questions as to the deterrent impact of the death penalty. To simplify, economists (e.g., Shepherd[11] and Zimmerman[12]) argue that the death penalty deters while most criminologists (e.g., Berk[13] and Donohue and Wolfers[14]) argue that it does not deter. The National Academy of Sciences has reviewed the debate and concluded that there is no clear answer at this point in time.[15] So believers cannot point to any research that unequivocally affirms a deterrence claim. Second, the weight of the scientific evidence is that the death penalty does not save money; in fact, it is more expensive than a life sentence.[16] A study of Indiana's practices showed that the average cost of a death penalty trial and direct appeal (almost four hundred thousand dollars) was approximately ten times the cost of a trial and appeal where the maximum sentence is life without parole (about forty thousand dollars).[17] Third, it is impossible to single out the "worst of the worst," those murderers who are so vile that it is without question that they deserve the death penalty. For example, Donohue did a study in Connecticut that demonstrated that eight of the nine murderers on death row had committed murders less vicious than 35 murderers who were not on death row.[18] Fourth, since 1973 two hundred murderers have been exonerated after being sentenced to death.[19] In other words, it is clear that juries can and do err at times in voting for the death penalty for someone whom the prosecutor labeled a vile murderer but who in fact did not commit the crime. Additional defendants may have indeed killed a victim but for various reasons do not legally qualify for the death penalty. In other words, there may be mitigating factors such as having suffered child abuse that mitigate against that individual legally deserving the death penalty.

Furthermore, proponents of the death penalty for adults and life without parole for juveniles point out the viciousness of many murderers. Heritage Foundation authors **Stimson and Grossman** describe sixteen horrific murders committed by juveniles as evidence for this position. For

11. Shepherd, "Deterrence Versus Brutalization," 203–256.
12. Zimmerman, "Estimates," 909–941.
13. Berk, "Can't Tell," 845–851.
14. Donohue and Wolfers, "The Death Penalty," Article 3.
15. Nagin & Pepper, *Deterrence*.
16. Bohm, *Deathquest*.
17. Death Penalty Information Center, "Indiana Death Penalty."
18. Donohue, "An Empirical Evaluation," 637–696.
19. Death Penalty Information Center, "Facts."

example, one youth told his friend that he needed some money and was going to steal it. He proceeded to approach a woman and her daughter in their car as the mother was making an ATM withdrawal to buy ice cream for her daughter and herself on a summer evening. The youth shot the mother and the same bullet also killed the daughter. These Heritage Foundation authors make a straightforward claim: horrendous acts of violence and cruelty are the worst harms individuals can inflict.[20] What is missing is the fact that many adults and juveniles who murder had childhood backgrounds of abuse and neglect. For example, a study of 1,579 juvenile lifers found that many had suffered from socioeconomic disadvantages, school failure, and abuse. Specifically, 79 percent had witnessed violence in their homes, almost half (47 percent) had been physically abused, and 77 percent of the girls had been sexually abused. About one-third were raised in public housing, and 18 percent were not living with a close relative just prior to their incarceration. Only 47 percent had been attending school at the time of their offense, and 84 percent had been either suspended or expelled from school at some point in their past.[21] A horrific childhood does not justify murder but it raises questions whether the murderer deserves to die.

THEOLOGIANS ON THE DEATH PENALTY

Just as the Catholic Church and the Southern Baptist Convention offer diametrically opposed statements on the death penalty, so too theologians can and do disagree. H. Wayne House takes the view that the death penalty is perfectly compatible with both the Old and New Testaments of the Bible:

> The biblical evidence for capital punishment may be summarized with these observations. In Genesis 9 God establishes a covenant with all humanity in which, among other things, he gives mankind permission to exercise judicial authority among themselves to exercise his wrath against the crime of murder....Nothing in the teachings of Jesus or the apostles contradicts this sanctioning [of capital punishment]. Capital punishment is a proper course of action for governments today in the exercise of their divine mandate to punish evil.[22]

---

20. Stimson and Grossman, "Adult Time."
21. Nellis, "The Lives of Juvenile Lifers."
22. House, "The New Testament," 422.

THE DEATH PENALTY

Going beyond biblical specifics, House focuses on the idea that all humans are made in the image of God. A murderer wipes out a particular expression of God's image. Therefore that murderer should pay an appropriate penalty. The death penalty respects the dignity of both the victim and the murderer.[23]

John Howard Yoder, however, takes a more aspirational view of what the Bible, especially what Jesus, has to say about capital punishment. He argues that Jesus came to set up higher standards, to go beyond what had been. For example, Yoder notes that in the story of the woman caught in adultery, when Jesus said that he who is without sin cast the first stone, Jesus was saying that "the judge and the executioner must be morally above reproach….[Thus] The Christian challenge to the death penalty properly begins where Jesus does, by challenging the self-ascribed righteousness of those who claim the authority to kill others."[24]

Furthermore, the life and redemptive death-resurrection of Jesus make a difference, including a difference in how society should deal with sinners/lawbreakers:

> …we are learning that the saviorhood of Jesus applies to law, and to social punishment for sin, no less than to prayer. Jesus as the forgiver of sin not only removes sin's power over the sinner's behavior but also its power to dictate guiltiness and demand punishment."[25]

Yoder also makes some pertinent comments about Romans 13, which many, for example, the Southern Baptist Convention, rely on as endorsement of capital punishment. Yoder interprets Romans 13 as authorizing punishment in general "but there is not specification of the content of the citizenship or the 'punishment.'"[26] Second, Paul's use of the word "sword" (*machaira*) does not refer to the arm of the executioner but is a symbol of judicial authority. Third, it is incorrect to assert that in Romans 13 Paul was delivering guidelines for Roman civil society. Christians were "an infinitesimal minority within Roman/Mediterranean culture, there was no place for them to contemplate immediately effective social critique."[27]

---

23. House "The New Testament," 415–28.
24. Yoder, "Noah's Covenant," 438.
25. Yoder, "Noah's Covenant," 438–439.
26. Yoder, "Noah's Covenant," 442.
27. Yoder, "Noah's Covenant," 443.

HELP FOR QUESTIONING CHRISTIANS

Thus, whereas House emphasizes the death penalty as a proper punishment for a person who has freely committed a horrible wrong and deserves proper punishment, Yoder sees Jesus calling for Christians to challenge the world

> one point at a time, to take one step in the right direction, to move up one modest notch in approximation of the righteousness of love....Thus the Christian (and any believer in democracy) will be concerned to restrain the violent, vengeful potential of the state. That potential for violence does not need our advocacy; it is already there."[28]

Collins (2019) takes a slightly different perspective. First, he notes that the Old Testament "prescribes capital punishment with alarming frequency."[29] In fact, the Hebrew Bible authorizes it for hitting your parents (Exod 21:15), for a child who is rebellious (Deut 21:18–21), and for both participants in adultery (Lev 20:10). As for Jesus and the New Testament, Collins does not see Jesus opposing the death penalty although he did mitigate "the severity of the [Old Testament] law in some respects."[30] Collins concludes that "opposition to the death penalty receives scant support from the Bible....[In fact,] [t]he Bible provides plenty of precedents, but it does not compel anyone to follow those precedents."[31]

Collins also argues that the Bible itself teaches the "changeability of divine law."[32] He cites the example of Deuteronomy 15:12 changing Exodus 21:7 from commanding the release of male slaves after six years to also apply to female slaves. Collins also notes Jesus claiming authority in the Sermon on the Mount to change laws given to Moses on Mt. Sinai and concludes "is it not possible to envision further changes in light of vastly different circumstances between the biblical period and our own time?"[33] Parenthetically, this is what Catholic teaching on the death penalty has done. It has noted that Old Testament times did not have lengthy prison sentences as an available option. In twenty-first century America, however, we have prison sentences available that can protect society from murderers

---

28. Yoder, "Noah's Covenant," 440.
29. Collins, *What Are Biblical Values?*, 47.
30. Collins, *What Are Biblical Values?*, 49.
31. Collins, *What Are Biblical Values?*, 50.
32. Collins, *What Are Biblical Values?*, 13.
33. Collins, *What Are Biblical Values?*, 13.

committing new crimes. So this is an example of "vastly changed circumstances" justifying changes in the ethics of capital punishment.

Theologians do not have a great deal to go on. Jesus did not issue a formal teaching on capital punishment. True, he did intervene with the woman accused of adultery but scholars take different positions on whether this implies that Jesus favors the death penalty (e.g., compare House versus Yoder). Some see Jesus as not condemning the Jewish use of capital punishment for adultery. Others see Jesus as dealing with one woman in a particular fashion without intending to enter any debate on the merits of the death penalty in general.[34]

One theologian with a unique slant on this issue is George Boyd. Boyd argues that if Christians really want to show their respect for human life, the best way to do that is to abstain from taking the lives of murderers:

> To respect human life precisely where its bearer has forfeited personal claim to that respect would be society's ultimate statement both of the sanctity of life and of the kind of society it wants to be. Undeniably, the reciprocity of killing as punishment for murder in its own way takes life very seriously; but two side effects undercut its impact. Achieved reciprocity implies a new *equilibrium, a state of justice achieved or restored, but the taking of an* innocent life cannot be compensated, any more than a jealous lover's act of murder is morally neutralized by a self-punishing suicide. *Murderers should never be allowed the comfort of the illusion that they can "pay" for their crime.*[35]

So again here is an issue that sincere Christians disagree on. Is it not troubling that sincere Christians can differ on such an important matter? If Southern Baptist preachers and church leaders are correct, the state should be executing and probably executing more frequently than current practice. If Catholic leaders, including the Pope, are correct, then the death penalty is clearly immoral.

How does God allow for two diametrically opposed positions on such a life and death matter? It is understandable that God might allow believers to differ on less serious matters. For example, Catholics practice individual confession to a priest whereas Protestants teach that believers should confess their sins and repent for them in the privacy of their prayer conversations with God. In one sense, this variation does not matter. Both Catholics

---

34. See, e.g., Prejean, *Dead Man*.
35. Boyd, "Capital Punishment," 163.

and Protestants believe that believers should repent and refrain from future sin. Theologically, if believers do this, they will end up in heaven. So the belief difference does not affect the ultimate destination of the believer: heaven.

The issue of the death penalty has even influenced a judge on the U.S. Supreme Court. The late Antonin Scalia was a strong proponent of the death penalty. When the Supreme Court ruled that the death penalty is unconstitutional for the mentally challenged and for juveniles, he wrote dissents in both cases.

He discussed his opposition to the death penalty in light of his Catholicism. As noted above, both the U.S. Catholic Bishops and the Pope have written that the death penalty is not consistent with Christian teaching. Normally a conservative like the late Justice Scalia would be predicted to be an ardent supporter of religious teaching. But in this case, Scalia thought that both the Bishops and the Pope had deviated from more traditional Catholic teaching. He argued that earlier Church teaching had it right in endorsing capital punishment and that relatively recent Church teaching was an aberration from the truth.[36] He was correct that Church teaching had changed. In his view, that change was an aberration; in the view of two Popes and the U.S. Catholic Bishops, that change was an example of the rightful evolution of Church teaching.

Consider the import of Scalia's position. If in fact not only is capital punishment authorized but is even authorized for the mentally challenged and for juveniles, consider the ramifications. If this is true, one could argue that Jesus would be comfortable with executing mentally challenged persons and youths who kill! One factor that is particularly egregious with juveniles is that their youthful immaturity can be held against them. Prosecutors tend to argue that if a youth has committed murder, that is especially dangerous because starting so young portends a future of more horrendous actions unless they are stopped as soon as possible!

To sum up, several Christian bodies have issued formal resolutions or statements on the death penalty, both pro and con. So preachers who follow the directives of their churches may themselves preach pro or con sermons. Theologians can also be pro (e.g., House) or con (e.g., Boyd; Yoder). Or one could cite Collins for the position that the Bible offers non-compelling precedents in favor of capital punishment. Criminologists, for the most

---

36. Scalia, "God's Justice," 17–21.

part, have opposed the death penalty. They have based their opposition on lack of evidence of deterrence, high costs, and numerous mistakes.

Thus believers can favor or oppose the death penalty and find support for either stance in official church documents and also from theologians. On the other hand, if Christian are looking for support from criminologists, for the most part it is not there. The overwhelming number of criminologists oppose the death penalty due to lack of evidence of deterrence, high costs, an inability to identify the "worst of the worst" murderers, and a significant number of errors in past cases.[37] The major dissenting voice in social science academic circles is a cadre of economists who, one, see support for the deterrent impact of the death penalty and, two, therefore favor the death penalty because they think it does save lives.

Going a bit astray, going further into detail than perhaps necessary, it is intriguing to note that one economist in the support camp is Zimmerman. Zimmerman's research found evidence of a deterrent impact—but only when the electric chair is the means![38] Also finding evidence of deterrence is Shepherd—but only if a state executes frequently enough![39] For the sake of argument, let's say both economists are correct. That would mean that for there to be a deterrent effect, a state would have to use the electric chair instead of lethal injection *and* execute frequently. States, however, are no longer using electrocution and many states do not execute that frequently. So states are not following what two economists say would produce a deterrent effect.

In conclusion there are theologians who will back up those preachers who wish to preach the death penalty. There are economics professors who will do the same. But there are both theologians and church leaders, including both the U.S. Catholic Bishops and two Popes who have called for the end of America's fascination for and employment of the death penalty. And the majority of criminologists concur.

LIFE SENTENCES

As states are imposing fewer death sentences and also executing fewer persons on death row, life sentences, including life without parole (LWOP), are replacing death sentences. As of 2020 161,512 prisoners were serving life

---

37. See Bohm, *Deathquest*, for a full discussion of these issues.
38. Zimmerman, "Estimates," 909–41.
39. Shepherd, "Deterrence," 203–256.

sentences. Another 42,353 prisoners were serving virtual life sentences. A virtual life sentence is a sentence of fifty years or longer, that is, a sentence so long that in all likelihood the sentenced prisoner will die in prison.[40] Life sentences have been mushrooming due to the punitive climate that began in the 1980s. Fears about rising crime rates led to harsh sentencing measures such as three strikes and you're out laws which led to many of these life sentences. The reasoning was that three-time violent felons deserved such a harsh sentence and that it would prevent a fourth or fifth crime. But at times one or more of the three strikes for alleged dangerous offenders are not violent crimes. Life without parole sentences have even been given out for shoplifting from a department store and siphoning gasoline from a truck![41] Also, reluctance to prosecute some murderers as capital murderers and perhaps jury reluctance to vote for a death sentence are additional reasons for more life sentenced prisoners.

To focus on just one state, Louisiana has over four thousand prisoners serving life sentences without the possibility of parole, accounting for 15 percent of the state's prison population. Between 1995 and 2020, Louisiana added an average of one hundred and ten persons annually to its total of life-sentenced individuals.[42]

On the one hand, it would seem that a life sentence is a good answer to many of the problems with the death penalty. For example, a life sentence can allow for mistaken convictions to be corrected years after a mistake was made in court. An execution, however, means that newly discovered evidence cannot correct a mistaken death sentence. Also, a life sentence is a severe punishment and all agree that the serious crime of murder deserves a severe punishment.

On closer examination, however, life sentences are not problem-free. Some criticize life sentences for being the equivalent of the death penalty. Feld calls a life sentence "a slower form of death."[43] Johnson and McGunigall-Smith call a life sentence "America's other death penalty."[44] The argument is that a life sentence means that the offender will die in prison, so that makes it a "death penalty." Related to this argument, a life sentence means a lifetime in prison with no hope for redemption. One study of prisoners

---

40. Nellis, *No End in Sight*.
41. ACLU, "A Living Death: Life Without Parole for Nonviolent Offenses."
42. Nellis, *Life in Prison*.
43. Feld, "A Slower Form," 9–65.
44. Johnson & McGunigall-Smith. "Life without Parole," 328–346.

serving life sentences found that many felt that their sentence confirmed that they were failures and that there was no way to repair the damage they had done.[45] Henry agrees: "The offender is forever branded and banished and often will reach old age or die in prison without ever having the opportunity to prove that he or she has been transformed."[46]

On the other hand, one study on life without parole inmates indicated that the initial time of their sentence is stressful. After some time, however, the stress and even mental health symptoms decline. In fact, after a period of time serving such as sentence, many are able to be "active agents in creating purpose and finding meaning in their lives"[47]

Parenthetically, it is interesting that many religious people favor the death penalty. Although the concept of redemption is at the heart of Christianity—Christ died for the redemption of the sins of all humans—many believers cannot find it in their hearts to accept any possibility of redemption for murderers. So it appears that many Christians accept redemption for themselves but are not open to redemption, at least in this life, for murderers. So Jesus' instruction to forgive seven times seventy (Matt 18:12) apparently does not apply to the sin of murder.

Contrary to the argument that the death penalty or a life sentence offers no hope, one can point to some prisoners who do find some sort of meaning even on death row or even while serving a life sentence. One such person is Jarvis Masters who has found Buddhism in prison and who has even written a book about his positive personal transformation in prison.[48] He is a living example of how one can find meaning and purpose even in the horrible situation of awaiting one's execution.

Some might point out that Masters has always insisted on his innocence and is fighting his fate. That can be considerably different from the situation of a prisoner who does not maintain his or her innocence and has to face up to the fact that he/she committed a horrible murder and society has condemned him or her to execution or life without parole. Also, although an exceptional individual such as Masters may be able to find meaning while awaiting execution or serving a life sentence, that does not mean that most such prisoners will be able to do the same.

---

45. Johnson & McGunigall-Smith. "Life without Parole," 328–346.
46. Henry, "Reducing Severe Sentences," 400.
47. Leigey, "For the Longest Time," 247–268.
48. Masters, *Finding Freedom*.

Another problem with the proliferation of life sentences is that life sentences do not inspire lawyers and concerned citizens to step up and volunteer to help the prisoners appeal their sentences. Death sentences, because death is final and ultimate, motivate both lawyers and concerned citizens to help death row inmates appeal their sentences. Life sentences, because they do not come with an expiration (execution) date, do not inspire the same commitment to volunteer and work on appeals. A lawyer might think that prisoner X does not deserve the death penalty, the most extreme penalty available. So the lawyer would be willing to work on an appeal. With a life sentenced inmate, a lawyer might think that the sentence is too harsh but that the prisoner does deserve some punishment, perhaps twenty years. Given a prisoner who deserves twenty years, that lawyer might not be quick to appeal a life sentence. The sentence may be seen as excessive but not as egregious as a death sentence.

Another issue with life sentences is that at some point they lose any utilitarian value. If a life sentence is meant to serve the utilitarian end of incapacitation, after fifteen or twenty years they fail to deliver. As offenders age, their propensity to commit crime gets closer and closer to zero. This is especially clear after age fifty.[49] So at some point a life sentence serves little or no utilitarian purpose but only serves a punitive purpose.

Given the severity of life sentences, it would seem that an ethical criminal justice system would only impose the death penalty or a life sentence in the most limited fashion. Tonry, for example, suggests that LWOP sentences only be given for first-degree murder otherwise punishable by death.[50] The American justice system has been using the death penalty less and less in recent years but resorting to life sentences more and more. Both sentences send a message to offenders that their lives are empty of meaning and worth.

Unlike the case with the death penalty, church bodies and theologians have not been issuing resolutions or academic treatises on life without parole sentences. However, as criminologists have equated a life sentence with a death sentence (recall Feld and Johnson and McGunigall-Smith above), it follows logically that our discussion of the death penalty also applies to life sentences, especially life without parole. In other words, by equating life sentences with the death penalty ("a slower form of death"), criminologists have indicated that any religious/theological discussion of the death penalty

---

49. Henry, "Reducing Severe Sentences," 397–405.
50. Tonry, "Remodeling American Sentencing," 503–533.

therefore applies to life sentences. So it would be logical for Catholics, for example, to oppose and for Southern Baptists to favor such sentences.

In 2000 the Catholic Bishops issued a statement "Responsibility, Rehabilitation, and Restoration: A Catholic Perspective on Crime and Criminal Justice." In this statement they began by noting that "the current trend of more prisons and more executions...does not truly reflect Christian values."[51] Then they rejected simplistic solutions to the crime problem including three strikes and you're out laws and rigid mandatory sentencing. So it appears that the Bishops reject at least some life sentences, namely, those for a third strike. They also emphasized the importance of rehabilitation and criticized states that abolished parole. So, although the Bishops did not go so far as to explicitly rule out all life sentences, their statement does seem to say that they are not in favor of the current proliferation of life sentences to two hundred thousand plus and counting.

A crucial point, however, is that religious bodies and theologians may not agree with the criminologists who equate life sentences with capital punishment. If a religious body or a theologian sees a life sentence as instead qualitatively different from a death sentence, then either could logically support such life sentences.

So a Catholic who is staunchly pro-life might oppose the death penalty but embrace a life sentence as an acceptable alternative. This hypothetical Catholic might not be acquainted with or agree with the contention of writers like Feld that a life sentence is the functional equivalent of a death sentence. As noted above, a death sentence is dramatic: often a life ends at the symbolic hour of midnight! A life sentence also ends a life but the end is a long, drawn out quasi-existence in a prison that can extinguish the human spirit over decades instead of at the injection of a needle of life-ending drugs.

CONCLUSION

A Christian trying to determine the morality of the death penalty faces a daunting task. Two major churches, the Southern Baptist Convention and the Catholic Church, differ on this issue. The SBC supports capital punishment while the Catholic Church now opposes it. Similarly, one might argue that the Old Testament supports the death penalty while the Gospels (and Jesus) do not explicitly address the issue.

51. USCCB, "Responsibility."

A possible avenue to resolve this conflict is Yoder's contention that the SBC's reliance on Romans to endorse the death penalty is erroneous. Yoder notes that Romans endorses governmental authority in general but does not specifically endorse the death penalty. The Catholic Church, on the other hand, emphasizes Jesus's teaching on forgiveness as its basis for opposing the death penalty.

Given the absence of any endorsement of the death penalty by Jesus, one could argue that contemporary criminologists assert that the evidence indicates that either the death penalty does not deter or there is lack of evidence in favor of deterrence, that mistakes occur, that it is difficult to determine the worst of the worst who deserve capital punishment, and that capital punishment is both time-consuming and costly. As a result, the consensus of most criminologists is opposition to the death penalty.

Although life sentences might appear to be a simple alternative, some criminologists point out that such sentences actually share the problems of the death penalty. The Catholic Church explicitly opposes the death penalty and rejects simplistic solutions, thereby raising serious reservations about life sentences.

CHAPTER 10

Religion and Politics: From Presidential Elections to Christian Nationalism to "Let Them Eat Cake"

"Christian nationalism idealizes a mythic society in which *real* Americans—white, native-born, mostly Protestants—maintain control over access to society's social, cultural, and political institutions, and 'others' remain in their proper place."—Andrew Whitehead and Samuel Perry

"We recognize, O Lord, that in Thy sovereignty Thou has permitted Richard Nixon to lead us at this momentous hour of our history."—Billy Graham

"So God made Trump."—Truth Social

INTRODUCTION

THE ELECTION AND PRESIDENCY of Donald Trump and recent United States Supreme Court decisions have brought several ethical issues to the forefront for Christians. First, can a Christian support a candidate for President who has apparently lived, at best, a questionable ethical life? Does that candidate's support for political positions that a Christian supports outweigh any concerns one might have about the candidate's personal ethics? Is support for critical issues such as the pro-life position on abortion so important that a Christian might even feel obligated to vote for him or her?

Second, and related to the first, how far should Christians push their ethical beliefs in the political realm? Many think that the United States is a Christian nation and that God wants Christians to fight for political and cultural choices based on Christian values. Many Christians, for example, believe that their religion forbids abortion and that there should be a federal ban on abortion following the recent Supreme Court overturning of *Roe v. Wade*. Others emphasize separation of church and state. Sociologist Andrew Whitehead[1] and others frame this discussion as one about white Christian nationalism and its effects on American politics, economics, education, and culture.

Third, can a Christian's stance on certain ethical issues exempt the Christian from performing a service or doing business with individuals who oppose the supposed "Christian" position? For example, can a Christian feel free to not service or do business with gay individuals in certain circumstances such as baking a wedding cake for two gay individuals who are about to marry? If Catholics think that sterilization (vasectomies and tubal ligations) are sinful, can Catholic hospitals refuse to perform such procedures? What if they are the only medical facility in the area and patients cannot afford to go elsewhere?

CHRISTIANS AND ELECTIONS

As citizens, the case can be made that Christians have an ethical obligation to keep informed and vote for the best candidate for elective office. In 2016 Donald Trump ran for President and promised to promote several pro-Christian agenda items such as nominating judges for the Supreme Court who would be pro-life. In 2016 evangelicals responded with overwhelming support and were a key to his election. He followed through with three Supreme Court nominees who later overturned *Roe v. Wade* and thereby made abortion a state-by-state issue. And the former President reached out to evangelicals for support in the 2024 election.

Both as a candidate and as President, Donald Trump exhibited very questionable, if not appalling, behaviors. During debates he insulted other candidates, even ridiculing personal appearance. He lies repeatedly about almost everything. During his presidency, he made over thirty thousand false or misleading claims.[2] He insults prosecutors and judges who try him

---

1. Whitehead, *American Idolatry*.
2. Washington Post online fact-checker.

on charges. He spoke of treating women in sexually derogatory ways. He has been sued and found liable for sexual assault and defamation.[3] His tweets insulted and stoked hatred rather than uniting the country in common goals. He has been indicted on multiple felony charges, convicted in New York, but apparently spared further action due to his re-election. He denied the legitimacy of the 2020 election and he stirred up the emotions of the rioters who invaded the Capitol on January 6th. Many say he supported an insurrection.

So a Christian who votes for Donald Trump can feel positive that he or she is voting for a pro-life, anti-abortion candidate who in fact nominated the Supreme Court judges who overturned *Roe v. Wade*. A Christian nationalist agrees with Trump's anti-immigrant and anti-refugee position. On the other hand, that Christian is also voting for an inveterate liar who has been accused of attacking the very foundations of American democracy such as abiding by election results and facilitating the peaceful transition of power. Prior to his re-election in 2024, Trump was facing several trials for his actions following the 2020 presidential election. Furthermore, Trump has proven himself to be questionable at best as a businessman. A court ruled that he had to pay "graduates" of Trump University twenty-five million in damages for real estate courses that did not deliver as promised. Trump is notorious for allegedly not paying debts but forcing people who do work for him to sue to try to get paid. The civil trial in New York alleged that he grossly overvalued his properties to obtain bank loans.

A particularly disturbing aspect of Trump's candidacy and then his Presidency is his claim to "Make America Great Again." The disturbing aspect is the implicit or explicit racism associated with this claim. The "Again" word in the phrase signifies taking America back to an earlier time when things were "great." A problem with this return to an earlier age is that much of our history is tied in with slavery, Reconstruction, and Jim Crow. For much of our history, blacks have been slaves or subject to discrimination and structural inequality. (For an analysis of he impacts of race on the criminal justice system, see Alexander[4] or Currie.[5]) Slavery existed from our founding to the Civil War. Immediately following the Civil War, blacks appeared to be on a better track, including being elected to political office. But Reconstruction turned back into suppression of blacks, including being

---

3. Fea, *Believe Me*.
4. Alexander, *The New Jim Crow*.
5. Currie, *A Peculiar Indifference*.

blocked out of voting and economic and social suppression. Jim Crow is a history of the South treating blacks as inferior beings who were intimidated into humiliating demonstrations of homage to the "superior" white citizenry. The Civil Rights Movement ended Jim Crow but structural inequality continues. So black Americans do not think that going back to earlier times is desirable or honorable.

In short, as will be shown in the section on Christian nationalism, a vote for Trump may be a vote against abortion but it is not a vote for true Christian values. But many Christians rationalized their support of Trump in 2016 due to his promise and action to end abortions in the United States. In 2024 many voters apparently felt that concerns abut immigration, inflation, and the economy outweighed any ethical concerns. Or perhaps they objected to Democrats' pledge to push against any abortion restrictions. Such Christians offer Trump a pass for actions and speech that they would most likely condemn in any other President.

HISTORY

This issue of how closely a Christian should identify with political candidates and office holders is far from new. Pope Pius XII faced this very issue in the late 1930s through the 1940s as he sought to be a moral spokesperson at the same time that his country, Italy, had a fascist leader, Mussolini, who joined forces with the Nazi leader, Adolf Hitler. Several points are critical. On the one hand, the Pope and the Catholic Church at the time perceived Communism under Stalin to be the archenemy of the Catholic Church in particular and religion in general. On the other hand, the Pope saw Mussolini as sympathetic to Catholicism. Similarly, the Pope was carrying on secret negotiations with Hitler in an effort to get Hitler to soften his stance against the Catholic Church in Germany. But while the Pope was trying to get Hitler to be more positive to German Catholics, the Pope also was getting disturbing reports about Hitler's harsh treatment of both Jews and Polish Catholics. The Pope chose not to speak out directly against Hitler's murdering of both Jews and Polish Catholics, despite numerous pleas from various sources to do so.[6] So a religious leader, a Catholic Pope, wound up remaining silent about one of the most egregious moral outrages of all history, the Holocaust, and he supported Italy's alliance with the author of the Holocaust.

6. Kertzer, *The Pope*.

In the United States, we have had a President, Eisenhower, who took action to overthrow legitimate governments in countries such as Iran and Guatemala.[7] Similarly, Presidents Johnson and Nixon waged a war in Vietnam that pitted a troubled, to say the least, regime against an enemy that argued that it was fighting for national sovereignty versus foreign powers. Further, there were clear indications that the United States would never win the war but both President Johnson and Nixon kept the war going for political reasons. Specifically, Henry Kissinger and President Nixon finally signed a truce that had essentially the same terms that were available four years earlier.[8] Neither wanted to be discredited for "losing" a war!

The complete picture of what our presidents perpetrated concerning regime changes and in waging war in Vietnam took decades to uncover. Yet at the time various religious leaders endorsed Presidents Eisenhower, Johnson, and Nixon. For example, Billy Graham became almost an advisor for President Nixon.

The lesson seems to be that both religious leaders and voters who are church members need to be wary of too close an entanglement with or support of any president or political leader. For one, presidents do not always reveal exactly what they are doing. It may take years or decades for historians to uncover all that President X did while she was in office. Thus, a religious leader or voter who supports a particular political leader may be totally ignorant of what that leader is actually doing behind the scenes. It was not until the transcripts of the President's tapes came out that voters would learn of Nixon's anti-Semitic remarks, for example.

Also, just because a President is a member of a particular church, that does not mean that he is a good Christian or a good Jew or Muslim. John F. Kennedy was a Catholic but his dalliances with numerous women indicate that he did not take Catholic teaching on sexual ethics very seriously. Richard Nixon courted evangelical voters but his actions in the Watergate scandal show that his primary concern was getting and keeping political power, no matter the cost. He also pursued his "Southern strategy" which critics have attacked as racist. Lyndon Johnson had two affairs long before he became president.[9] Donald Trump courted Christian voters by promising and nominating judges who would overturn *Roe v. Wade* but his personal sexual ethics are far from Christian and his leadership and failure

7. Hitchcock, *The Age of Eisenhower*.
8. Brigham, *Reckless*.
9. Caro, *Master of the Senate*.

to concede the 2020 election results have divided the country. Candidate George W. Bush promised "compassionate Christianity" and actually set up an office to carry out his promise. But as many soon learned, President Bush was not that concerned about carrying out his promise. He made the promise to garner votes.

It seems that the prudent course of action for religious leaders is to maintain some distance between themselves and politicians. Yes, they can point out that candidate X supports a position that their church or Christian principles supports. But any close identification with a candidate runs the risk that that candidate may not be all he or she claims to be and that that candidate can become a president or senator or governor who actually carries out unchristian and even godless actions.

The same advice applies to ordinary churchgoers who are voters; just because a candidate supports one or more positions that are important to Christians, you may not know all that there is to know about that candidate's positions or eventual actions in office. It may take years for voters to learn that the person they voted for did something completely unethical or that that person was racist, anti-Semitic, or something similarly repugnant.

CHRISTIANITY AND CULTURE: WHITE CHRISTIAN NATIONALISM

To phrase the issue as whether or not Christians should vote for a person such as Donald Trump who, to say the least, has questionable ethics, is to miss the true nature of the problem. The reality is that a sizable number of Christians have adopted a mindset, Christian nationalism, that allows them to see a Donald Trump as not only acceptable but as a champion of Christian values. In January 2024 Trump supporters even aired a video entitled "God made Trump" which claimed that God intended since 1946, the year of Trump's birth, for him to lead the United States along the path that God wants. So a significant proportion of Christians are supporters of Christian nationalism and that worldview is one that sees Donald Trump as a defender of both Christianity and American patriotism. In this frame of reference, Christianity and patriotism are so linked that adherents believe that God is intervening in American history and politics. Even when Trump ends his second term, Christian nationalists will continue to believe that religion and politics are linked and they will simply transfer their present allegiance to Trump to the next politician who espouses their mindset.

A primary researcher on Christian nationalism, Andrew Whitehead, defines the phenomenon as:

> a cultural framework that idealizes and advocates for a fusion of a particular expression of Christianity with American civic life. It holds that this version of Christianity should be the principal and undisputed cultural framework in the United States and that the government should vigorously preserve that cultural framework.[10]

Whitehead's research shows that just under half (49 percent) of Americans embrace Christian nationalism. But most evangelical Protestants (78 percent) are Christian nationalists, as are about 50 percent of mainline Protestants and Catholics.[11] So Christian nationalism characterizes most evangelicals and about half of mainline Protestants and Catholics.

Christian nationalists trace their beliefs to the founding Fathers. Christian nationalists hold that the Founding Fathers were traditional Christians who based the Constitution on Christian principles. The problem is that this point of view is erroneous:

> But this story is a myth. The religious views of the Founders ranged widely: from atheism through deism and Unitarianism to Congregationalism, Baptism, and even Roman Catholicism. The Declaration and the Constitution drew on various influences, including classical liberalism (e.g., Locke) and civic republicanism (e.g., Machiavelli). More than a little of the nation's wealth and prosperity were derived from stolen land and slave labor. These are all well-established facts.[12]

A major problem with Christian nationalism is that it is linked with racially discriminatory attitudes, support of police efforts to control minorities, negative views toward immigrants, and militarism in international affairs. For example, the more one embraces Christian nationalism, the more likely they state that they are "not at all comfortable" with their daughter marrying a black man and show lower support for transracial adoption. Christian nationalists are less likely to not believe that slavery was the central cause of the civil war and more likely to oppose the removal of Confederate monuments and statues of former slave owners.[13] Christian

---

10. Whitehead, *Christian Idolatry*, 28–29.
11. Whitehead and Perry, *Taking America*.
12. Gorski and Perry, *The Flag*, 102.
13. Gorski and Perry, *The Flag*.

nationalists are much more likely to believe that police treat blacks the same as whites and that police officers who shot blacks did so because blacks are more violent than whites. Christian nationalists are more likely to support restrictions on voting such as requiring voters to pass a civics test and keep those who committed certain crimes from voting. They also tend to see Muslims and even atheists as threats to American values and institutions.[14]

A quite troubling aspect is its support for violence:

> Violence can be understood as an attempt to maintain proper order when (implicitly white) police or "good guys with guns" wield it against (implicitly non-white) "bad guys." It can even be read as an attempt to restore order as in the Capitol insurrections. But it is viewed as moral degradation and dystopian chaos when attributed to Black Lives Matter, Antifa, or the inhabitants of inner cities. White violence is the ultimate source of order; Black or leftist violence, by contrast, is the ultimate source of disorder.[15]

All agree that police and the military have the right to use force when appropriate. But the Christian nationalist support for violence helps explain how George Zimmerman shot and killed Trayvon Martin in Florida and how Kyle Rittenhouse shot three men, two fatally, in a disturbance in Kenosha, Wisconsin as well as the insurrection of January 6th.

To summarize:

> Christian nationalism idealizes a mythic society in which *real* Americans—white, native-born, mostly Protestants—maintain control over access to society's social, cultural, and political institutions, and "others" remain in their proper place. It therefore seeks strong boundaries to separate "us" from "them," preserving privilege for its rightful recipients while equating racial and religious outsiders with criminality, violence, and inferiority.[16]

The crux of the matter is that *Christian* nationalism does not actually embrace *Christian* values:

> Put simply, Christian nationalism does not encourage high moral standards or value self-sacrifice, peace, mercy, love, justice, and so on. Nor does it necessarily encourage conforming one's political opinions to those that Jesus might have....Rather, Christian nationalist appeals to "Christian foundations" and "Christian beliefs"

---

14. Whitehead and Perry, *Taking America*.
15. Gorski and Perry, *The Flag*, 102.
16. Whitehead and Perry, *Taking America*, 118–119.

were more like code words for a way of life that is "ours" (read: white conservative Christians) by divine right and which "the secularists, the humanists, the atheists, the infidels" want to take away.[17]

In other words, Christian nationalism is not Christian, it embraces positions that Jesus would not.

Columnist David French offers a more moderate take on Christian nationalism than Whitehead. French claims that only 10 percent of Americans are *committed Christian nationalists*. However, he also notes that they seem to be able to influence more moderate Christians and that such influence can be critical in elections, including presidential elections. He also emphasizes that Christians have the right to fight for their values but their worldview cannot rule out other views and values:

> The problem with Christian nationalism isn't with Christian participation in politics but rather the belief that there should be Christian *primacy* in politics and law. One can welcome Christian participation in the public square while resisting domination from any faith or creed.[18]

French's distinction between participation and domination is one that resonates with American democracy but not necessarily with Christian beliefs. Politically, America has a government that is built on majority rule with respect for the minority. Christian beliefs often say that God commands X and forbids Y, such as the belief of many Christians that abortion is murder and therefore sinful. So both Christian nationalists and many other Christians do not see how they can allow for abortion. So while French says Christian participation in the public square is legitimate, many Christians, including Christians who are not Christian nationalists, are not open to allowing women, for example, to obtain abortions but want a national ban on abortion.

Sociologist Andrew Whitehead is also a committed Christian. As such, he suggests that Christians can do several things to fight racism and thereby atone for past racism on the part of Christians or their failure to confront racism. First, in response to wealth gaps between whites and blacks, he calls for white Christian denominations to give portions of their wealth to minority denominations, schools, and congregations. This could

---

17. Whitehead and Perry, *Taking America*, 86.
18. French, "Christian Beliefs."

entail foregoing efforts to increase their own size and influence. Second, "[s]ocial contact that fosters engagement and interaction and learning is equally important. Majority white congregations and organizations will need to develop true bonds of relationship."[19] Third, white Christians need to vote for policies and politicians that support redressing racial inequalities in health, wealth, and educational opportunity. Fourth, Christians need to oppose any expressions or existence of white Christian nationalism in their denominations or churches. In sum, Whitehead calls on Christians to realize that the message of Christ goes beyond individual salvation to include economic and racial equality:

> We can embrace the gospel of Jesus that realigns the power structures of society that crush those on the margins, a gospel that disrupts systems of oppression and their destructive effects on human relationships. We can embrace the gospel that Jesus came so we *all* might have life abundant.[20]

Similarly, Whitehead also questions the antipathy of white Christian nationalists toward immigrants and refugees:

> I wonder how we might respond to Jesus if he asked about our love for our neighbors. I have the sense that we might echo the lawyer's reply to Jesus in the Gospel of Luke, seeking to justify ourselves in the face of our inaction: "And who is my neighbor?" (10:29).[21]

Whitehead suggests several courses of action to help immigrants and refugees. First, vote for candidates who would enact policies to help them. Second, donate your time or money to organizations "focused on ensuring that immigrants and refugees can live and work in peace rather than fear for their safety."[22] In general, "We can begin to look for where and how we can listen and learn and then stand with those on the margins."[23]

In other words, Whitehead is a far cry from someone who wants to build a wall on the border and keep out all immigrants and refugees. Instead, he cites the command of Christ to love our neighbor to include immigrants and refugees.

---

19. Whitehead, *American* Idolatry, 154.
20. Whitehead, *American* Idolatry, 157.
21. Whitehead, *American* Idolatry, 162.
22. Whitehead, *American* Idolatry, 177.
23. Whitehead, *American* Idolatry, 177.

WEDDING CAKES, WEBSITES, AND GAY MARRIAGE

The Supreme Court has ruled that the First Amendment prevents a Christian baker from having to bake a wedding cake for a gay couple about to get married. In *Masterpiece Cakeshop, Ltd. v. Colorado Civil Rights Commission et al.* decided in 2018, the Supreme Court ruled that the baker's claim that a wedding cake he created would express an endorsement of gay marriage, contrary to his religious beliefs.

The dissent noted that the gay couple simply requested the baker to bake a wedding cake; they asked for no message on the cake. For the dissent, the baker was refusing to provide a good or service to a same-sex couple that he would provide to a heterosexual couple. If the couple were a nonwhite heterosexual couple, Phillips' refusal would be a clear case of racial discrimination.

In *Creative LLC et al. v. Elenis et al.* decided on December 5, 2022 Justice Gorsuch ruled in favor of website designer, Ms. Smith, who refused to design a website for a gay couple. Gorsuch argued Ms. Smith wished to create wedding websites only for couples whose marriages she endorsed. In this case, the state of Colorado was forcing her to create a website for a marriage her conscience told her is wrong. So Ms. Smith is protected by the First Amendment from being forced to engage in such speech.

Judge Gorsuch went on to note that if the Court ruled against Ms. Smith, that could lead to forcing a religious Muslim to make a film with a Zionist message or forcing an atheist artist to paint a mural celebrating evangelical zeal. It could even lead to the sadly ironic case of forcing a male website designer married to another man to create a website for an organization that actually advocates against same-sex unions.

In her dissent, Justice Sotomayor argued that the Court ruling gives a business open to the public the right to refuse to serve members of a protected class because the owner of the business believes that same-sex marriages are false. So the dissent sees the issue as discrimination, not one of free speech. Justice Sotomayor argues that the Constitution "contains no right to refuse service to a disfavored group." In other words, public accommodations laws ensure that all citizens, regardless of race, sex, and so on have the right to be served by a public business. Colorado added marital status to what constitutes a matter for pubic accommodation.

Justices Gorsuch and Sotomayor both make compelling arguments. Both free speech and refusal to discriminate are critical values in our nation's history. Since Justice Gorsuch wrote for the majority, his opinion means that a religious person does not have to engage in speech contrary to his/her religious beliefs, even if that denies a service to a gay couple getting married. A recent action by Pope Francis, however, suggests that despite the ruling of the Supreme Court, a Christian perhaps ought to provide the service in question.

IMPLICATIONS OF CATHOLIC CHURCH BLESSINGS OF SAME-SEX COUPLES ON THE ISSUE OF BAKING A WEDDING CAKE OR CREATING A WEBSITE FOR A GAY COUPLE

In December of 2023 Pope Francis authorized priests to confer a blessing on same-sex couples.[24] While this is *not* an approval of such unions nor an indication that the Church will allow same-sex couples to enter into sacramental marriage, it signifies a softening of attitude toward such unions. It also raises an interesting question vis-à-vis the Supreme Court rulings that bakers and website creators do not have to sell their goods or services to gay couples planning to get married.

Since the Pope is saying that a priest can bless a same-sex couple, can a Catholic refuse all goods/services to such a couple? Does the Pope's allowance of a blessing for a gay couple indicate that the Catholic Church is not 100 percent opposed to such unions? If so, how can a Catholic baker or website creator claim that his/her conscience does not permit the believer to serve the gay couple clientele? Does the authorization of such blessings suggest that a baker or a website creator can offer their services to a gay couple without that service indicating that the baker/website maker is endorsing the marriage? The Pope seems to be indicating that a priest can confer a blessing without that blessing meaning that the Church or the priest heartily endorses the union. If Jesus were on earth to rule on this issue, would he endorse the baker/website creator for standing up for the sanctity of traditional marriage? Or might Jesus say, "Two gay persons want to express their love for one another and making a cake or a website does not in and of itself mean that the baker or the Internet guru gives his/her personal stamp of approval on the issue of gay marriage?" Given Jesus' criticisms of the Pharisees for being sticklers of the Jewish law, one guess is He might well say, "It's not that big a deal."

24. Winfield, "Activists Hope."

RELIGION AND HEALTHCARE

Catholic hospitals, of course, refuse to provide abortions. Given that Chapter 7 discusses the issue of abortion and given that abortion is such a fundamental issue for all including medical providers and hospitals, here we will discuss a medical issue for Catholic hospitals that many non-Catholics might not even be aware of, namely surgery to prevent having a child. Catholic hospitals have a policy of not performing procedures such as vasectomies or tubal ligations. It is plainly spelled out in the ethical directives of the U.S. Conference of Catholic Bishops: "Direct sterilization of either men or women, whether permanent or temporary, is not permitted in a Catholic health care institution."[25] The President of the National Catholic Bioethics Center calls such surgery "a silent moral plague" and a "grave violation of sexual ethics."[26] The Christian ministry Focus on the Family, however, states that the Bible does not address this modern medical issue and declines to weigh in:

> As representatives of a non-denominational ministry, it is not our goal to make pronouncements in this part of the debate over contraception. If you're wrestling with questions of this nature, we recommend that you discuss them with your pastor or priest.[27]

So if an individual, Catholic or non-Catholic, wants to be sterilized, he/she must choose a non-Catholic hospital. Thus, the interest/right of an individual to request a legal medical procedure is pitted against the right of a religious hospital to refuse to perform procedures that its religion considers immoral. It is important to note that 76 percent of Americans state that surgery to prevent having children is an *appropriate* use of technology.[28] Recall that 62 percent of Americans say that abortion should be legal.[29] So three-quarters of Americans see such surgery as appropriate but Catholic hospitals refuse to offer the surgery. In other words, Catholic hospitals refuse to provide a procedure that most American see as appropriate. A related issue is that doctors trained in Catholic hospitals will not get training in

---

25. USCCB, "Ethical and Religious Directives."
26. Meany, "The Silent Plague."
27. Focus on the Family, "Practical, Moral."
28. Funk et al., "From Plastic Surgery."
29. Blazina, "Key Facts."

tubal ligations, a popular method of birth control as about seven hundred thousand sterilization ligations are performed annually.[30]

One study found that doctors working in Catholic hospitals disagreed with strict prohibition of sterilizations, especially when denying a tubal ligation placed the patient at increased medical risk. Cesarean delivery in Catholic hospitals raised frustration for obstetrician-gynecologists when the hospital prohibited a simultaneous tubal ligation and, thus, sent the patient for an unnecessary subsequent surgery. Obstetrician-gynecologists described some hospitals allowing tubal ligations in limited circumstances.[31] Yet these same Catholic hospitals accept public funding (Medicare and Medicaid).

EXTENT OF RELIGIOUS INFLUENCE

A critical question behind many of these specific issues is to what extent should religion influence life in the U.S.? For example, now that the Supreme Court has thrown out *Roe v. Wade*, pro-life advocates and legislators are using religious reasoning in many of the states that are passing or have passed anti-abortion laws. The laws state that God is the author of life, that the Bible condemns abortion, and so on. Opponents contend that such arguments represent imposing religious beliefs on everyone.

COMMON FEATURES

These issues—religion in politics, freedom to not bake a wedding cake for a gay wedding, whether a patient in a Catholic or Baptist hospital can get a procedure such as a vasectomy—share a common thread. Conservatives, including many Christians, worry that a liberal agenda is spreading in the United States. Liberals, including Progressive Christians, see conservatives trying to hang on to traditional beliefs and moral points of view that liberals see as no longer tenable.

Some label this as a culture war and they are correct. It is a fight between two opposing worldviews. Conservatives seek a return to the 1950s or the 1800s where almost all agreed that abortion, premarital sex, and homosexuality were sinful and wrong. Liberals disagree. Conservatives do

---

30. Martin, "U.S. Bishops."
31. Stulberg, et al., "Tubal Ligation," 422-428.

not overtly call for any return to racism but there appear to be currents of racism just below the surface for some on the right. There appears to be concern that America is ceasing to be a white, Christian nation. Population trends bear this out.

CONCLUSION

Christians' support of Donald Trump is perplexing and problematic. It is perplexing that followers of Christ support a man who does not exemplify the values of Jesus in his actions. It is problematic for the many who see him as a threat to democracy. History teaches us that presidents often sinned, especially by conducting extra-marital affairs. More serious is the fact that history teaches us that it may take years or decades to uncover the full truth about presidential actions, from the real reasons for involving the nation in wars to how a president was involved in the overthrow of legitimate governments because he thought that was the best course of action for America.

Sociologist Andrew Whitehead and others, however, frame the issue in broader terms. Almost 80 percent of evangelical Christians and half of both mainline Protestant and Catholics embrace Christian nationalism, a framework that sees America as a Christian nation with God involved at the founding and at present. Most troubling is that Christian nationalism does not embrace true Christian values such as justice and love but instead

> Christian nationalism idealizes a mythic society in which *real* Americans—white, native-born, mostly Protestants—maintain control over access to society's social, cultural, and political institutions, and "others" remain in their proper place. It therefore seeks strong boundaries to separate "us" from "them," preserving privilege for its rightful recipients while equating racial and religious outsiders with criminality, violence, and inferiority.[32]

Some would respond that they believe that America has corrected its racist past and that all Americans, black and white, now have equal opportunity to succeed. Chief Justice Roberts took this approach in ruling against affirmative action in college admissions in *Students for Fair Admissions, Inc. v. President and Fellows of Harvard College*, 2023. In fact, he noted that affirmative action at Harvard had discriminated against both Asian-American and white applicants by reducing the numbers of both groups admitted.

---

32. Whitehead and Perry, *Taking America*, 118-19.

Specifically, Justice Roberts was concerned that Harvard's policy on race resulted in 11.1% fewer Asian-Americans being admitted to the university. Justice Roberts, however, made no mention of the fact that in 2017 almost one million young blacks, age 16 to 24, were "disconnected," meaning that they neither had a job nor were enrolled in school.[33] Justice Roberts and many Americans appear to believe that the days of systemic or implicit racism are over and that the current issue is reverse discrimination against whites and Asian-Americans. Whitehead would argue that this Supreme Court ruling is one example of how the power structure that Christian nationalists support poses problems for black Americans.[34]

It would be wonderful if the assessment of Chief Justice Roberts in *Students for Fair Admissions*...were indisputable: all discrimination except reverse discrimination is a thing of the past. Reality, however, indicates that systemic racism, economic inequality, and structural disadvantage are still with us. Christians can choose to believe, like Justice Roberts, that discrimination and racism are past history, or recognize the problems that still exist and try to follow Jesus and address those problems.

Parenthetically, Justice Roberts had a father who was a plant manager of the Bethlehem Steel plant in Burns Harbor, Indiana. Roberts grew up in a wealthy upper class family, even going to a Catholic boarding school in La Porte, Indiana and then Harvard undergrad and Harvard Law School. One wonders how he would view the issue of racial discrimination if he grew up only a few miles away in South Chicago, the son of a family struggling to get by, and he had to attend a public school in a neighborhood racked by crime!

Andrew Whitehead and others go beyond Trump to depict how widespread and deep the problem of Christian nationalism is. If you believe that God founded the United States as a Christian nation and the He basically anoints someone like Donald Trump at birth to later lead America back to Christian values, it becomes impossible to see the true nature of such a politician. You become willing to support a man who was found liable for sexual assault, has told constant lies and hateful insults, and has been accused of actions that could destroy democracy. And the deeper issue is that Christian nationalism will not go away when Trump goes away. Others will take his place.

33. Currie, *A Peculiar*.

34. Whitehead, *American Idolatry*. For insightful discussions of the continuing problem of racism in the United States, see Alexander, *The New Jim Crow*, Hannah-Jones et al., *The 1619 Project*, and Ray & Mahmoudi, *Systemic Racism in America*.

Perhaps worse than preventing Christians from rejecting a man like Trump, white Christian nationalism serves to blind many Christians from seeing the need for efforts to work for social justice and to end racism. It comforts white Christian nationalists that they have risen to positions of wealth and power through their own hard work and allows them to dismiss social inequality as the failure of the poor and of blacks to work as hard as whites do. And it allows them to take a hard line against immigrants and refugees instead of seeking to follow a path inspired by Christian love.

Since Christian nationalists see God as instrumental in the founding and the ongoing fate of America, it becomes difficult to argue on policy and direction. If you believe that God is on your side, it is hard to consider the possibility that you may be wrong. In French's terms, Christian nationalists want more than mere participation in the public sphere, they want domination.[35]

Finally, it is critical to note that the problem is more than just Christian voters' support of one man. The problem is that Christian nationalism serves as an identity for millions of Americans. So the solution is to foster a new identity. Whitehead and Perry suggest a possible identity:

> These Americans may respond to a narrative of national identity highlighting the importance of religious freedom, rather than Christianity alone, and strength through diversity rather than privileging one religious tradition.[36]

In other words, our history has included values beyond the pale of Christian nationalism and now is the time to redirect the national mindset.

---

35. French, "Christian Beliefs."
36. Whitehead and Perry, *Taking America*, 158.

CHAPTER 11

Conclusion: Where Do We Go from Here?

"In other words, doctrine also progresses, expands and consolidates with time and becomes firmer, but it is always progressing."—Pope Francis

"The Christian movement is not a monolithic or fixed tradition, but rather a rich plurality of dynamic, often conflicting Christianities deeply divided over a host of issues, including sex, the role of women, and the diversity of family patterns."—Ellison

Snoopy's Theology Book Title: *Has It Ever Occurred to You That You Might Be Wrong?*

INTRODUCTION

ALTHOUGH OFFICIAL CHURCH PRONOUNCEMENTS (including a 2024 *Declaration*[1] by the Catholic Church) and many preachers and Christians consider abortion, physician-assisted suicide, premarital sex, hell, and other issues settled questions, scholars have presented credible alternatives. Reputable theologians and scholars in other disciplines have advanced theological, philosophical, legal, and scientific arguments that do present something different from what many preachers and many churchgoers think might be the only viewpoint. When a preacher or even a formal church resolution

---

1. Dicastery for the Doctrine of the Faith, *Infinite Dignity*.

proclaims that God ordains the death penalty, that euthanasia is murder, that eternal damnation definitely awaits the sinner, that hell awaits the gay person who dares to defy church teaching and engage in sexual activity with another gay person in a committed relationship, we have shown that there are theologians and, in appropriate instances, criminologists, law professors, philosophers, and psychologists, who take a different position. And there are churches that disagree with other churches about critical moral issues.

Consequently, the average believer can conclude that issues one thought settled, actually are open to debate for theologians and other scholars. The average believer, then, can consider these debates and decide to continue with a traditional answer or conclude that a fresh approach is better. The average believer can also have a clearer understanding of Christians who question traditional teaching.

Similarly, traditional churches, at the very least, need to address these issues anew. They need to respond to the alternative theological, philosophical, or social science arguments that assert that in some circumstances, abortion, premarital sex, homosexual intimacy, and physician-assisted suicide are permitted or even clearly moral choices. Traditional churches cannot simply assert that X is sinful without addressing recent scholarship. On all of the issues discussed in this book, scholars have presented logical, evidence-based positions that, at the very least, need to be considered by traditional churches. Simply dismissing recent writing ignores the fact that many believers already have abandoned traditional teachings or have gone to the extreme of now claiming they belong to no church. It also ignores the dramatic splits in several church bodies over issues such as treatment of gay church members and pastors.

RECENT DEVELOPMENTS

As noted in the discussions of homosexuality, abortion, and premarital sex, it is also important to point out that substantial percentages of churchgoers are ignoring what their preacher preaches on Sunday and what their church teaches in official pronouncements. While Catholic, Southern Baptist, and other Christian preachers and church resolutions say that homosexual sexual activity, abortion, and premarital sex are sinful, many Americans disagree. Seventy-one (71) percent of Americans have said that gay or lesbian relations are morally acceptable; 52 percent have said that abortion is morally acceptable; 76 percent have said that sex between an unmarried man and woman is morally acceptable. Furthermore, a majority of Americans (55 percent) think that physician-assisted suicide is acceptable.[2] Depending on how many churchgoers are involved, these statistics indicate that there are significant numbers of believers who do not follow the moral pronouncements they hear on Sunday or the official positions of their church. For example, over half (60 percent) of U.S. Catholics support legal abortions.[3]

It is also intriguing and disturbing that the churches are not in harmony. The Catholic Church opposes the death penalty while the SBC claims that the Bible calls for capital punishment. Divorce is not a settled issue. Both the Catholic Church and the SBC condemn abortion while the Evangelical Lutheran Church in America states that abortion is actually "morally responsible" where there is "a clear threat to the physical life of the woman." Second, abortion is permissible in cases of rape and incest and in "some situations in which women are so dominated and oppressed that they have no choice regarding sexual intercourse and little access to contraceptives." Third, abortion may be the responsible choice in "circumstances of extreme fetal abnormality, which will result in severe suffering and very early death of an infant."[4] Similarly, the Presbyterian Church USA states that abortion may be "morally acceptable" in problem pregnancies.[5] Both the Catholic Church and the SBC condemn homosexual sexual activity, that is, gay persons engaging in any form of sexual intimacy. For millions of Christians same-sex marriage is not open to debate as God clearly intended only traditional marriage between one man and one woman. On the other hand, the Presbyterian Church USA recently issued formal statements allowing LGBTQIA+ persons to both serve in church ministry and request a service of Christian marriage in states that allow same-sex marriage.[6]

Many Christians, especially those in conservative denominations, may have little awareness that other denominations take such positions on abortion or homosexuality and same-sex marriage. Hopefully, this book can inform them so that they have a better understanding of why other

---

2. Brenan, "Americans Say."
3. Blazina, "Key Facts."
4. Evangelical Lutheran Church in America, "A Social Statement on Abortion."
5. Presbyterian Church USA, "Abortion/Reproductive Choice Issues."
6. Presbyterian Church (USA), "What We Believe: Sexuality."

CONCLUSION: WHERE DO WE GO FROM HERE?

Christians are making choices that Christians in conservative churches thought were settled once and for all.

In Chapter 1 we noted the trend of people changing their religious identification from "Christian" to "none." If some of those dropping their identity as Christian do so because of questions about traditional moral teachings, they can take solace from the views of the scholars laid out in this book. The scholars' explanations serve as evidence that such Christians have legitimate concerns about traditional teaching. Those scholars show that it is possible to disagree with traditional teaching that automatically condemns homosexual sexual activity, premarital sex, physician-assisted suicide, and abortion. Those scholars indicate that the issues are more nuanced and that there is room for debate, not simple blind obedience. If church leaders were open to at least looking at some of this scholarship, one could have hope that they might be open to some changes. That hope, however, is rather minimal as churches have a history of being dogmatic, of taking a position and not being willing to even consider change. Both the Catholic Church and the Southern Baptist Convention appear to take dogmatic positions (see, e.g., *Infinite Dignity*, 2024[7]) and do not appear willing to even allow for questions and discussion.

WHERE WE ARE: SUMMARY OF ANALYSES

The following summary outlines the current status of the issues discussed in the book. (Note: For cites, see prior chapters.)

The Prosperity Gospel: While Prosperity Gospel promoters such as Joel Osteen do offer Scripture quotes to support their message, it appears that most theologians see Jesus as preaching a message of detachment rather than abundance. Furthermore, the Bible also directs believers to assist their fellow humans rather than blame the needy for their economic state.

Hell: Several churches persist in a traditional view of hell as both eternal and as involving considerable torment. Rabbi Blech and Rasmussen, a philosopher, however, argue for either a time limit on hell or for its nonexistence. Historian Bart Ehrman contends that Jesus taught that sinners do *not* go to hell but are destroyed.

Heaven: The Catholic Church offers the least controversial view, namely, that a complete picture of heaven is not possible, that heaven is a mystery. Alcorn has written what he claims is a Bible-based account of

---

7. Dicastery for the Doctrine of the Faith, *Infinite Dignity*.

heaven that paints it as a five-star resort complete with golf and travel. N. T. Wright advises us to put less emphasis on the afterlife and more emphasis on working to establish the Kingdom of God by working for good and justice right now. Mark Twain's humorous tale of heaven raises critical objections to stereotyped depictions; not everyone wants to just stand around singing hymns or playing the harp all day and each of us has our own idea of what would be perfect happiness,

Death Penalty: It appears that the Catholic Church is on sounder Scriptural ground in its opposition to the death penalty than the SBC's citing of Paul's Letter to the Romans. The message of Jesus does seem to be one of love and forgiveness rather than any emphasis on punishment. Furthermore, the fact that most criminologists see no utility and considerable economic and social cost in the death penalty is strong reason to reject the death penalty in the twenty-first century.

Physician-assisted Suicide: Both Jesus and the Bible more generally never addressed this issue as it was not an issue until about two millennia after Jesus. A traditional approach is that God decides when we die. The other approach is to argue that the New Testament focuses on a God of love who does not demand every last moment of suffering. The Catholic Church uses the principle of double effect to assert that pain killers that eventually cause death are ethical because their primary effect is to end pain and death is a permissible secondary effect. A film such as *The Suicide Tourist* offers a compelling case for an individual who has suffered for some time with ALS to have the right to decide that enough is enough. Traditionalists, however, argue for the redemptive aspect of suffering.

Abortion: Traditionalists cite references in the Bible about God considering us in the womb and even before as evidence that life begins at conception and abortion is wrong. Nontraditional scholars disagree about alleged biblical support for a pro-life stance. Pro-choice scholars both disagree that personhood begins at conception and emphasize respect for a woman's right to make choices about her own body. Kamitsuka offers a strong argument that there is no evidence that the Parable of the Good Samaritan instructs pregnant women to birth and then raise a fetus to adulthood. She also offers a thorough discussion of the personhood issue, recognizing fetal value but also recognizing the mother's right to abort.

Pre-marital Sex: The traditional answer is that sex is confined only to traditional marriage of a man and a woman. Writers such as Peters see that the changed circumstances of contemporary life call for allowance for sex

CONCLUSION: WHERE DO WE GO FROM HERE?

in committed relationships such as that of two graduate students in college or perhaps two senior citizens, one of whom is married to a person with Alzheimer's. Some go further and see sex as a positive part of life and hence something that can be pursued quite openly, as long as each party respects the other party.

Homosexual Sex and Gay Marriage: The traditional approach is that the Bible shows God as sanctioning only heterosexual sex and traditional marriage. Scholars such as Collins do not see a biblical condemnation of homosexual sex. One can argue that the biblical focus on love and on the truth that humans are not meant to be alone is a way to argue for gays to marry and to express their sexuality. At least two churches have adopted this view.

Divorce: On many of the issues discussed in this book, churches, especially conservative churches, take a hard line approach that the question is clearly settled: abortion, homosexual sexual activity, and physician-assisted suicide are sinful. Concerning divorce, however, these same churches admit the strict teaching of Jesus on the indissolubility of marriage but open the door for compassionate treatment of the many Christians who marry but later feel they can no longer stay married.

Politics: For many believers and for many media pundits, the puzzling question is how can those who call themselves Christians support a former President, now a re-elected President, who, at best, lives a questionable ethical life? Sociologist Whitehead and others, however, argue that the problem is more complex. Many Americans, Christian and secular, embrace a perspective, Christian nationalism, that embraces racism, rampant capitalism, anti-immigrant views, and even violence. Critics argue that Christian nationalism seeks to perpetuate white privilege in a country that is becoming a minority white nation. Whitehead suggests the remedy is to turn away from trying to preserve privilege and to turn to true Christian values such as love, mercy, and justice.

WHERE WE ARE GOING: IMPLICATIONS

The major implication of this analysis is that a Christian trying to make ethical decisions has both traditional answers as set forth in church pronouncements and the nontraditional answers of recent scholarship. In fact, several churches take a nontraditional approach on some of these issues. A believer can consider both points of view and decide for himself/herself which course of action is right. If the believer chooses to continue with the traditional answer, he/she can do so stronger in faith because one has looked at other points of view and decided that the traditional answer is the best answer. If the believer opts for one of the views of recent scholarship, he/she can argue that recent scholarship supports his/her choice. This believer does not have to feel that her choice to disagree with official teaching automatically makes her a "sinner" or a "heretic." Instead, she can take comfort in the fact that at least one or more scholars has presented a credible argument for taking a position contrary to that of her church.

Another possibility is that an examination of recent scholarship may actually convince the person that the traditional position in fact is the better answer! Reading a new position may show the person that the newer position lacks sound reasoning and the best ethical course is the traditional approach. Or the new position may lead the person to consult scholars who hold the traditional approach and find reason there to opt for the traditional approach. As noted in Chapter 7, for example, Kaczor offers a book-length defense of the pro-life position in general including the specific point that human personal life begins at conception.[8]

Although churches such as the Catholic Church claim that official teaching is clear on certain issues, for example, abortion, other churches are more open to allowing each individual to decide, at least in certain circumstances. For example, the SBC has a history of proclaiming the priesthood of all believers, thereby giving importance to each believer. More generally, whatever Luther's original intention, the Protestant Reformation started a wave of individual churches, each with varying positions on what used to be settled doctrine. The Reformation implies that Christians can disagree with official teaching. Finally, recently Catholic Cardinal Reinhard Marx stated that the Catholic Catechism is not "set in stone" as he asked whether Catholics should regard an intimate relationship between two same-sex persons as "worthless."[9] Both Marx and other Cardinals think that the Catholic Church needs to reconsider its teaching on homosexuality and gay relationships. Similarly, Pope Francis recently stated that "we need to understand that there is an appropriate evolution in the understanding of matters of faith and morals."[10] The Pope cited the morality of slavery and the atomic bomb, both of which had been considered moral but now are

8. Kaczor, *The Ethics of Abortion*.
9. National Catholic Register, "Cardinal Marx," 2022.
10. Spodaro, "The Water Has Been Agitated."

CONCLUSION: WHERE DO WE GO FROM HERE?

sinful. Conservative Catholics no doubt will quickly insist that the Pope did *not* say that right and wrong are evolving but that our *understanding* is evolving. Also, some conservative Cardinals have noted their objections to some of the Pope's liberal views. This is not the place for a treatise on the evolution of dogma or moral teaching, but the Pope did state that we now understand that the death penalty and slavery are wrong (sins) whereas churches previously endorsed both. And as noted in Chapter 9, the Catholic Church did indeed change its position on the death penalty.

On the other hand, as noted in Chapter 1, in April 2024 the Catholic Church rejected gender theory, calling it a grave violation of human dignity, and also reiterated its opposition to abortion and euthanasia.[11] These pronouncements suggest that the Church has chosen to stand by earlier conservative statements and is not open to change on these issues. The Catholic hierarchy sincerely believes that its position on right to life is correct and is what God demands.

A second implication is that churches cannot expect to simply mandate moral choices with no concern for opposing viewpoints. On each issue examined in this book, scholars have presented reasonable alternatives to traditional teaching. To remain credible, churches must, at the least, address such positions before enunciating a directive. Churches need to realize that many of today's churchgoers are college graduates, many with advanced degrees. They are accustomed to thinking for themselves. Unlike centuries ago, churches cannot assume that the faithful are ignorant or uneducated. If a church wants to issue a moral statement, it needs to be well grounded in Scripture, theology, and if pertinent, philosophy or the social sciences. To fail to do so is to risk losing more church members to the "nones" mentioned in Chapter 1, the growing number of former church members who now claim no religious affiliation. Even Jesus seems to have focused on guiding principles (e.g., love of neighbor) rather than specific moral precepts. One might argue that He appears to leave it to each believer to apply "love thy neighbor" to concrete circumstances in the twenty-first century—some two millennia after His ministry.

A third implication is that Christians who look at new scholarship but decide to stay with traditional approaches will be better equipped to engage in honest dialogue with Christians and non-Christians who do not follow traditional teaching. Unless one is willing to consider why someone does not agree with you, it is impossible to have an honest discussion

---

11. Dicastery for the Doctrine of the Faith, *Infinite Dignity*.

with that person about how and why you differ. Unfortunately, the political landscape appears to generate partisan positions in which opponents will not even consider what the other side thinks. Religious issues, however, are so critical that there needs to be respectful and honest discussion. Several of the issues are life and death issues—abortion, the death penalty, and physician-assisted suicide. And Christians have the added life or death dimension of eternal life—heaven or hell.

A fourth implication is that both sides need to consider the possibility that their position is not as obvious and certain as they have always assumed. The analyses have shown that on all of the issues recent scholarship presents sound argumentation and evidence. Thus, positions considered beyond debate may in fact be debatable. At the very least, the analyses show that both sides need to admit that the other side has some basis and cannot simply be dismissed. Related to this, if it is logical or evidence-based to hold that abortion, physician-assisted-suicide, gay marriage, etc. are moral choices, then it does not seem appropriate to simply condemn those choices. Nor does it seem appropriate to engage in crusades against the other side. One can disagree but still respect the other side for being sincere in its stance.

The Catholic Church I attend and its associated Knights of Columbus Chapter hold "prayer opportunities" at a local abortion center several times a month. I would argue that the purpose is not so much prayer as it is to have a crowd of Christians show up at the clinic to try and make the women going to the clinic feel guilty about their choice. For those who do not want to go to that abortion center, there are prayer opportunities once a week at a Catholic cemetery. "Praying for life" is a logical consequence of the Catholic Church's position that abortion is clearly sinful. But prayer meetings at an abortion center where women who have made a thoughtful decision to seek an abortion are, of course, an attempt to put psychological and spiritual pressure on those women and on the health personnel staffing the center. If the demonstrators were to admit that perhaps there are sound arguments on the pro-choice side, perhaps they would be less ready to call for and participate in such actions.

Also, given Pope Francis's recent talk about new understandings of doctrines, traditional Catholics should allow for some possibility that positions they considered sacrosanct are not immutable. If the Pope and some Cardinals see some room for change, then average Catholics need to do the same. For example, *Washington Post* writer E. J. Dionne recently wrote about his position as a Progressive Catholic that the Church needs to re-examine its positions on divorced and LGBTQIA+ people, the ordination of women, and opening the priesthood to married men.[12]

As noted, the Catholic Church has shown signs of possibly being open to change. The recent Synod on Synodality noted that certain issues, such as "matters of identity and sexuality, the end of life, complicated marital situations, and ethical issues related to artificial intelligence," "raise new questions" and need "reflection" and "further clarification."[13] On the other hand, this position has been criticized by both bishops and theologians,[14] and the Vatican's recent document, *Infinite Dignity*, reaffirms traditional teaching on many matters.[15]

Some may prefer not to even consider questioning "settled" answers to moral issues. Some may prefer earlier times when believers looked to their pastor and their church body for *the answer* to each of the issues we have examined and did not even presume to question that answer. It can be troubling to question positions one has assumed are settled. Just as Socrates said that the unexamined life is not worth living, so also it seems that one's moral positions cannot be unexamined. If one thoughtfully analyzes moral issues and comes to a reasoned decision, it seems logical to think that God would judge that decision more positively than a decision to simply accept a church's traditional teaching without any questioning. If God gave us the power to reason, doesn't He want us to use that power?

DIFFICULTY OF ACCEPTING NEW VIEWS

Some of the implications of this examination of contemporary Christian ethics are easier to acknowledge and accept than others. Abolition of the death penalty, a softer stance on divorce, and agreeing that Jesus does not promise wealth to all are already accepted by many Christians and churches. Other implications are more controversial.

Abortion, for example, is a litmus test for many evangelical Christians and Catholics. As this is being written, the U.S. Supreme Court has overturned *Roe v. Wade*, a number of states have enacted prohibitions on abortion, and pro-life advocates are pushing for national restrictions

12. Dionne, "Opinion."
13. U.S. Conference of Catholic Bishops, *A Synodal Church*.
14. See Wiering, "Bishop Barron Criticizes Part" and Pentin, "The Synod."
15. Dicastery for the Doctrine of the Faith, *Infinite Dignity*.

on abortion. These actions are seen by evangelicals and Catholics as the fruit of decades of political effort to oppose *Roe*. Given decades of effort to overturn *Roe*, it is clear that these Christians will not be receptive to scholars such as Kamitsuka[16] and Peters[17] who present arguments for allowing abortion. Many Christians sincerely believe that life begins at conception or very early in the pregnancy. As noted in Chapter 7, Gutman and Moreno contend that the issue of when human life begins is irreconcilable and one about which both sides are absolutely inflexible.[18]

Opinion page writers such as Josh Hammer and Christine Flowers repeatedly proclaim their opposition to abortion. For example, Hammer recently lamented the vote in Ohio to deny a Republican initiative to require a 60 percent vote to amend the state constitution. Republicans wanted to make it more difficult to end any provision outlawing abortion. In his article, Hammer recognizes that a majority of Ohioans and Americans favor abortion being legal (within limits). Instead of respecting those views, however, he calls for pro-lifers to *educate* pro-choice persons to the position that life begins at conception and all abortions are immoral.[19] Similarly, Flowers takes traditional Catholic teaching as beyond debate.[20]

Similarly, the official newspaper of the diocese I live in, the Diocese of Knoxville's *The East Tennessee Catholic*, has frequent articles endorsing the pro-life position. For example, the November 2023 issue had an article about a woman who had an abortion but later realized the error of her ways and now speaks out against abortion.

The pro-life position is understandable. Even if one thinks that human life and personhood does not begin until some time after conception, the fetus or prenate, as Peters prefers to call it, will become a baby if allowed to develop. Also, as noted, couples begin to think of the fetus as their child very early in the pregnancy. Thus the pro-life stance is logical and emotional and has scholarly support. Readers are encouraged to study the issue thoroughly, including such pro-life scholars as Kaczor.[21]

Perhaps—but not necessarily the case—Christians might agree with McGlasson and Whitehead that Jesus does not call for a one-issue ethic.

16. Kamitsuka, *Abortion*.
17. Peters, *Trust Women*.
18. Gutman and Moreno, *Everybody Wants*, 61.
19. Hammer, "The Pro-Life Dilemma."
20. Flowers is a columnist for the *Delaware County Daily Times*.
21. Kaczor, *The Ethics of Abortion*.

CONCLUSION: WHERE DO WE GO FROM HERE?

Even though McGlasson does not approve of abortion, he reminds Christians that they are called to promote love and social justice, oppose any form of racism, and extend healthcare to all, not just to oppose abortion.[22] Whitehead calls for Christians to stop consoling Blacks with pictures of an idyllic afterlife and instead confront the racism that Christian theology both fostered and maintains.[23]

Concerning euthanasia, traditional believers offer arguments that a person can embrace even the horrendous suffering caused by a disease such as Lou Gehrig's disease. For example, a Catholic priest recently wrote an article about an ALS sufferer who continued to oppose and lobby against Washington State's assisted suicide initiative. The man insisted that despite the ravages of ALS he had a "marvelous quality of life" because he was surrounded by loved ones who cared for him.[24] The problem is that such traditionalists want everyone to take the same viewpoint, leaving no room for disagreement. But as with abortion, the traditional answer that euthanasia is wrong is understandable. Physician-assisted suicide does take a life and that goes against our normal choice to stay alive and keep our loved ones alive.

Homosexual sexual activity and same sex marriage are also hot button issues for many Christians. At the very least one would think that Christians could agree that Jesus does not condone or encourage any hate, whether hate speech or hateful actions. While some churches and theologians heartily embrace an ethic that sees nothing immoral with gay sexual intimacy and even gay marriage, it is clear that major churches (the Catholic Church and the SBC) see homosexuality as disordered and sinful. Time will tell where this debate leads but it seems that all Christians can agree that Jesus would not be speaking hate or condoning hate toward gay Christians.

It was only a few years ago that it was very popular for Christians to wear bracelets with WWJD inscriptions (standing for What Would Jesus Do?) on them. As pointed out in the specific chapters on abortion, euthanasia, and homosexuality, Jesus did not directly speak on these issues and there is debate over the Old Testament positions.[25] In other words, it seems that there can be room for even conservative Christians to move their thinking on these critical issues.

22. McGlasson, *Choose You This Day*.
23. Whitehead, *American Idolatry*.
24. Pacholczyk, "The 'Quality of Life' Error."
25. See Collins, *What Are Biblical Values?*

A major problem is that one's viewpoint on many of the issues discussed in this book is intimately intertwined with one's religious and cultural identity. One's stance on abortion, homosexuality, gay marriage, and premarital sex helps to define a person as a conservative evangelical or a liberal progressive or something in-between. Furthermore, that stance is often related to how an individual sees himself or herself as a Southerner or a Northerner, as working class or middle class, as a college graduate or a hard working non-college graduate, and as a believer in Jesus versus an atheist. These aspects of religious and cultural identity, moreover, have roots dating back to the founding of America. There is no illusion here that writing a book about what recent scholarship has to say about issues such as abortion, homosexuality, and premarital sex is going to suddenly overturn decades if not centuries of traditional beliefs. Nevertheless, one feels the need to point out what some scholars have written in the humble hope that some readers may find something to consider as they continue their religious journeys.

It would seem that traditional Christians would have an easier time changing on the issues that do not involve a life or death decision. Rejecting the Prosperity Gospel or coming to accept same-sex marriage does not involve any such decision. Accepting same-sex marriage, on the other hand, can be seen as very positive, as affirming the need for all persons to be able to enter a lifelong intimate relationship. As for the issues of abortion and euthanasia, it would seem that both sides can accept the absolute seriousness of these issues and respect the sincerity and good will of both sides while recognizing that neither side is likely to change course.

CONCLUSION

This book has discussed recent scholars who have presented positions that allow debate on a number of issues. The Catholic Church claims, for example, that the immorality of abortion is a closed issue. Recall, however, that the Catholic Church relatively recently changed its position on another life and death issue, the death penalty, from favoring it to condemning it for all intents and purposes. Recall that the late Antonin Scalia of the Supreme Court castigated the Church for this change of stance. So if a church body can change its mind on such a basic issue, arguably it can consider other changes too. As noted above, Pope Francis' recent statement that "we need to understand that there is an appropriate evolution in the understanding

CONCLUSION: WHERE DO WE GO FROM HERE?

of matters of faith and morals" and his note that slavery and the death penalty are immoral[26]—issues that once were considered moral—suggest that change of stance is possible. And recall that the Catholic Church held a Synod of Bishops in 2023 that stated that there is a need for both reflection on and clarification of several moral issues. On the other hand, the Vatican's recent document, *Infinite Dignity*, reaffirms traditional teaching on many issues[27] and appears to contradict any voices for change.

As noted, many Americans, including churchgoers, do not agree with traditional teaching that abortion, premarital sex, and physician-assisted suicide are immoral. Or at least they do not follow official teaching in their daily behavior or in what they tell opinion poll takers. In similar fashion, there are theologians and other scholars who both agree with those Americans and who also have presented plausible arguments to show why they think the way they do. Hopefully, this book will help readers to clarify their own positions, whether traditional or exploring new ground.

Two caveats: first, many individual believers and many churches firmly believe in traditional positions and see no need for any questioning. While this book endorses reflection, it respects those who choose not to question. The Pro-Life position on abortion, for example, resonates with the view of many parents that the discovery that a woman is pregnant means that "their child" is now growing! Second, this book does note some of the arguments for traditional answers but the focus is on alternative positions. So this book does not discuss how contemporary theologians who take traditional positions refute or might refute the arguments discussed here. The reader is advised to consult such scholars to get a complete picture. Readers are encouraged to seek out, for example, such pro-life scholars as Kaczor[28] before making their own decisions on such a critical issue as abortion or physician-assisted suicide.

Traditional Christians and Christian churches have performed great good in the world and will continue to do so. This writer thinks that questioning can help individuals and churches to get better but understands that individual believers and churches may think that some issues have been settled once and for all and that there is no need for questioning. The fact that many Christians say that they engage in or approve of behaviors condemned by their church and the fact that increasing numbers of Christians

26. Spodaro, "The Water Has Been Agitated."
27. Dicastery for the Doctrine of the Faith, *Infinite Dignity*.
28. Kaczor, *The Ethics of Abortion*.

appear to be saying that they no longer claim to be Christian suggest, however, that significant numbers of Christians/former Christians think that there is a current need for at least reflection, if not questioning. Perhaps traditional Christians need to look further into their traditional answers, find writers that clearly explain and justify such answers, and thus be ready to have further conversations with those who question traditional answers. This book is not intended to cause traditional Christians to question their beliefs. It is hoped, however, that traditional Christians try to have some understanding of believers who do question traditional answers. And questioning Christians need to think and examine their positions to be able to make the best decision, whether traditional or nontraditional. Both sides can benefit by reading theologians with traditional views and theologians with other views. One hope is that both sides can avoid demonizing the other but instead respect the good will of both sides.

Bibliography

Alberta, Tim. *The Kingdom, the Power, and the Glory: American Evangelicals in an Age of Extremism*. New York: Harper, 2023.
Alcorn, Randy. *Heaven*. Wheaton, IL: Tyndale House, 2004.
Alexander, Michelle. *The New Jim Crow: Mass Incarceration in the Age of Colorblindness*. 10th anniversary ed. New York: The New Press, 2020.
Allberry, Sam. *Is God Anti-Gay? And Other Questions about Homosexuality, the Bible, and Same-Sex Attraction*. London: The Good Book Company, 2015.
American Civil Liberties Union (ACLU). "A Living Death: Life Without Parole for Nonviolent Offenses." November 12, 2013. https://www.aclu.org/publications/living-death-life-without-parole-nonviolent-offenses.
American Psychological Association. (2008). "Answers to Your Questions: For a Better Understanding of Sexual Orientation and Homosexuality." https://www.apa.org/topics/lgbt/orientation.pdf.
Andone, Dakin, and Shawn Nottingham. "Southern Baptist Convention Votes to Uphold Removal of Saddleback Church Over Women Pastors after Appeal by Rick Warren." CNN, June 15, 2023. https://www.cnn.com/2023/06/14/us/southern-baptist-convention-annual-meeting/index.html.
Associated Press. "Southern Baptists Take Heat for Saying 46% in Alabama Are Bound for Hell." *Washington Post*, September 15, 1993. https://www.washingtonpost.com/archives/politics/1993/09/19/southern-baptists-take-heat-for-saying-46-in-alabama-are-bound-for-hell.
Banister, Nathaniel. "Being Gay Was No Longer Who I Was: This Hollywood Designer Met Jesus in a Supernatural Moment." The Christian Broadcasting Network, February 18, 2022. https://cbn.com/new/us/being-gay-was-no-longer-who-i-was-hollywood-designer-met-jesus-supernatural-moment.
Bell, Rob. *Love Wins: A Book about Heaven, Hell, and the Fate of Every Person Who Ever Lived*. New York: Harper One, 2001.
Berk, Richard. "Can't Tell: Comments on 'Does the Death Penalty Save Lives?'" *Criminology & Public Policy* 8 (2009) 845–851.
Blair, Gwenda. "How Norman Vincent Peale Taught Trump to Worship Himself." *Politico*, October 6, 2015. https://www.politico.com/magazine/story/2015/donald-trump-2016-norman-vincent-peale-213220/.
Blazina, Carrie. "Key Facts about the Abortion Debate in America." Pew Research Center, July 15, 2022. https://www.pewresearch/short-reads/2022/07/15/key-facts-about-the-abortion-debate-in-america/.

Bibliography

Blech, Benjamin. *Hope, Not Fear: Changing the Way We View Death.* Lanham, MD: Rowman & Littlefield, 2018.

Boer, Theo. "Dutch Experiences on Regulating Assisted Dying." *Catholic Medical Quarterly* 65(4) (2015) 25–26.

Bohm, Robert. *Deathquest: An Introduction to the Theory and Practice of Capital Punishment in the United States.* 5th ed. New York: Routledge, 2017.

Bowler, Kate. *Blessed: A History of the American Prosperity Gospel.* New York: Oxford University Press, 2013.

———. *No Cure for Being Human (and Other Truths I Need to Hear).* New York: Random House, 2021.

Boyd, George. "Capital Punishment: Deserved and Wrong." *The Christian Century,* February 17, 1988, 162–65.

Branstetter, Ziva. "Robert Tilton: From Downfall to Windfall: Living on a Prayer." *Tulsa World.* May 4, 2003. https://www.trinityfi.org/press/tulsaworld02.html.

Braswell, Michael, and John T. Whitehead. *Teaching Justice.* Carolina Academic Press, 2020.

Brenan, Megan. "Americans Say Birth Control, Divorce Most Morally Acceptable." Gallup, June 9, 2022. https://www.news.gallup.com/poll/3935/americans-say-birth-control-divorce-morally-acceptable.aspx.

Brigham, Robert K. *Reckless: Henry Kissinger and the Tragedy in Vietnam.* New York: Public Affairs, 2018.

Brooks, David. *The Road to Character.* New York: Random House, 2015.

Brownson, James V. *Bible, Gender, Sexuality: Reframing the Church's Debate on Same-Sex Relationships.* Grand Rapids, MI: Eerdmans, 2013.

Calabresi, Steven G. "How to Reverse Government Imposition of Immorality: A Strategy for Eroding *Roe v. Wade*." *Harvard Journal of Law & Public Policy* 31 (2008) 85–92.

Caro, Robert A. *Master of the Senate: The Years of Lyndon Johnson.* Vol. 3. New York: Knopf, 2002.

CBS News. "Euthanasia Deaths Becoming Common in the Netherlands." 2017. https://www.cbsnews.com/news/euthanasia-assisted-suicide-deaths-netherlands/.

Celebrity Net Worth Website. "Joel Osteen Net Worth." https://www.celebritynetworth.com/richest-celebrities/joel-osteen-net-worth/.

Collins, John J. *What Are Biblical Values? What the Bible Says on Key Ethical Issues.* New Haven, CT: Yale University Press, 2019.

Coogan, Michael. *God and Sex: What the Bible Really Says.* New York: Hatchette, 2010.

Cook, Becket. *A Change of Affection: A Gay Man's Incredible Story of Redemption.* Nashville: Thomas Nelson, 2019.

Currie, Elliott. *A Peculiar Indifference: The Neglected Toll of Violence on Black America.* New York: Metropolitan; Henry Holt, 2020.

Davis, Jim, and Michael Graham, with Ryan P. Burge. *The Great Dechurching: Who's Leaving, Why They Are Leaving, and What Will It Take to Bring Them Back?* Grand Rapids, MI: Zondervan Reflective, 2023.

Death Penalty Information Center. "Facts about the Death Penalty." November 2024, updated 2/3/25. https://dpic-cdn.org/production/documents/pdf/FactSheet.pdf?dm=1738593648.

———. "Indiana Death Penalty—Expensive, Unreliable, and Withering on the Vine." 2022. https://deathpenaltyinfo.org/commentary-indiana-death-penalty-unreliable-and-withering-on-the-vine.

Bibliography

deBellaigue, Christopher. "Death on Demand: Has Euthanasia Gone Too Far? *The Guardian*, January 18, 2019. https://www.theguardian.com/news/2019/jan/18/death-on-demand-has-euthanasia-gone-too-far-netherlands-assisted-dying.

Desmond, Matthew. *Poverty, by America*. New York: Crown, 2023.

Diamant, Jeff. "Half of U.S. Christians Say Casual Sex between Consenting Adults Is Sometimes or Always Acceptable." Pew Research Center August 31, 2020. https://www.pewresearch.org/short-reads/2020/08/3/half-of-u-s-christians-say-casual-sex-between-consenting-adults-is-sometimes-or-always-wrong.

Dicastery for the Doctrine of the Faith. *Infinite Dignity*. April 2, 2024. https://www.vatican.va/roman-curia/congregations/cfaith/documents/rc-ddf-doc-2024-04-02-dignitas-en.html.

Dionne, Jr., E. J. "Opinion: Pope Francis' Synod Is Radical – But Not in the Way His Critics Think." *Washington Post*, October 8, 2023. https://www.WashingtonPost.com/opinions/2023/10/08/pope-francis-synod-catholic-church/.

Donohue, John J. "An Empirical Evaluation of the Connecticut Death Penalty System since 1973: Are There Unlawful Racial, Gender, and Geographic Disparities?" *Journal of Empirical Legal Studies* 11 (2014) 637–96.

Donohue, John J., and Justin J. Wolfers. "The Death Penalty: No Evidence for Deterrence." *The Economists' Voice* 3 (5) (2006) Article 3.

Dulle, Colleen. "Explainer: What Pope Francis Actually Said about Civil Unions—and Why It Matters." *America*, October 22, 2020. https://www.americamagazine.org/faith/2020/10/22/pope-francis-gay-civil-union-lgtb-context-media-documentary.

Dworkin, Ronald. *Life's Dominion: An Argument about Abortion, Euthanasia, and Individual Freedom*. New York: Knopf, 1993.

Dworkin, Ronald W. *Artificial Happiness: The Dark Side of the New Happy Class*. New York: Carroll & Graf.

Edwards, Jonathan. "The Eternity of Hell Torments." Sermon, 1739. https://www.jonathan-edwards.org/Eternity.html.

———. "Sinners in the Hands of an Angry God." Sermon, July 8, 1741. https://www.jonathan-edwards.org/Sinners.html.

Ehrman, Bart D. *Heaven and Hell: A History of the Afterlife*. New York: Simon & Schuster, 2020.

Eldridge, Sherrie. *Twenty Things Adopted Kids Wished Their Adoptive Parents Knew*. New York: Dell, 1999.

Ellison, Marvin M. *Making Love Just: Sexual Ethics for Perplexing Times*. Minneapolis: Fortress, 2012.

Episcopal Church. "Heaven." In *An Episcopal Dictionary of the Church*. https://www.episcopalchurch.org/glossary/heaven/.

———. "Hell." In *An Episcopal Dictionary of the Church*. https://www.episcopalchurch.org/glossary/hell/.

———. *Summary of General Convention Resolutions on Abortion and Reproductive Health May 17, 2019*. https://www.episcopalchurch.org/ogr/summary-of-general-convention-resolutions-on-abortion-and-womens-resproductive-health/.

Evangelical Lutheran Church in America. "End of Life Decisions." November 9, 1992. https://elcamedicalresources.blob.core.windows.net/cddn/wp-content/uploads/End-Life-DecisonsSM.pdf.

———. "A Social Statement on Abortion." August 28, 1991. https://elcamedicalresources.blob.core.windows.net/cdn/wp-content/uploads/AbortionSS.pdf.

Bibliography

Farinas, Gerald. "What about Hell?" Edgewater Presbyterian Church Website. https://www.edgewaterpcusa.org./home/what-about-hell.

Fea, John *Believe Me: The Evangelical Road to Donald Trump.* Grand Rapids, MI: Eerdmans, 2018.

Feld, Barry C. "A Slower Form of Death: Implications of *Roper v. Simmons* for Juveniles Sentenced to Life without Parole." *Notre Dame Journal of Law, Ethics, & Public Policy* 22 (1) (2008) 9–65.

Fiala, Andrew. *What Would Jesus Really Do? The Power and Limits of Jesus' Moral Teachings.* New York: Rowman & Littlefield, 2007.

Focus on the Family. "Practical, Moral, and Spiritual Implications of Sterilization." March 28, 2023. https://www.focusonthefamily.com/family-qa/practical-moral-and-spiritual-implications-of-sterilizaition/.

French, David. "Christian Beliefs Are Welcome in Politics. Supremacy is Not." *Buffalo News*, February 24, 2024, A11.

Friedman, Ben M. *Religion and the Rise of Capitalism.* New York: Knopf, 2021.

Funk, Cary, et al. "U.S. Public Wary of Biomedical Technologies to 'Enhance' Human Abilities." Pew Research Center, July 26, 2016. https://www.pewresearch.org/internet/wp-content/uploads/sites/9/2016/07/PS_2016.07.26-Human-Enhancement=Survey-FINAL.pdf.

Gibson, David. "What Happens Now?" *Notre Dame Magazine* 50 (4)(Winter 2021-2022) 31-35.

Gorski, Philip S., and Samuel L. Perry. *The Flag and the Cross: White Christian Nationalism and the Threat to American Democracy.* New York: Oxford University Press, 2022.

GotQuestions.Org. "What Is Double Predestination?" https://www.gotquestions.org/double-predestination.html.

Griffith, R. Marie. *Moral Combat: How Sex Divided American Christians and Fractured American Politics.* New York: Basic, 2017.

Guida-Richards, Melissa. *What White Parents Should Know about Transracial Adoption.* Berkeley, CA: North Atlantic, 2021.

Gulley, Philip. *The Evolution of Faith: How God Is Creating a Better Christianity.* New York: HarperOne, 2011.

Gutman, Amy, and Jonathan D. Moreno. *Everybody Wants to Go to Heaven but Nobody Wants to Die: Bioethics and the Transformation of Health Care in America.* New York: Liveright, 2019.

Hannah-Jones, et al, eds. *The 1619 Project: A New Origin Story.* New York: One World, 2021.

Hardwig, John. "Dying at the Right Time: Reflections on Assisted and Unassisted Suicide." In *Is There a Duty to Die?*, 81–100. Hoboken, NJ: Wiley-Blackwell, 2020.

Haught, John F. *God and the New Atheism: A Critical Response to Dawkins, Harris, and Hitchens.* Louisville: Westminster John Knox, 2008.

Henry, Jessica S. "Reducing Severe Sentences: The Role of Prison Programming in Sentencing Reform." *Criminology & Public Policy* 14 (2015) 397–405.

Hitchcock, William I. *The Age of Eisenhower: America and the World in the 1950s.* New York: Simon & Schuster, 2018.

House, H. Wayne, ed. *Divorce and Remarriage: Four Christian Views.* Downers Grove, IL: InterVarsity, 1990.

Bibliography

———. "The New Testament and Moral Arguments for Capital Punishment." In *The Death Penalty in America: Current Controversies*, edited by Hugo A. Bedau, 415–28. New York: Oxford University Press, 1997.

Insights Journal. "Mike Murdock Net Worth." https://insightsjournal.co.uk/mike-murdock-net-worth.

Johnson, Robert, and Sandra McGunigall-Smith. "Life without Parole: America's Other Death Penalty. *The Prison Journal* 88 (2008) 328–46.

Jones, Jeffrey M. "Church Attendance Has Declined in Most U.S. Religious Groups." Gallup, March 25, 2024. https://news.gallup.com/church-attendance-declined-religious-groups.aspx.

Joseph, Daniel I. "What Do Methodists Believe about Heaven?" July 31, 2023. https://christianityfaq.com/methodists-believe-heaven.

Kaczor, Christopher. *The Ethics of Abortion: Women's Rights, Human Life, and the Question of Justice*. 3rd ed. New York: Routledge, 2022.

Kamitsuka, Margaret D. *Abortion and the Christian Tradition*. Louisville, KY: Westminster John Knox, 2019.

Kertzer, David. I. *The Pope at War: The Secret History of Pius XII, Mussolini, and Hitler*. New York: Random House, 2022.

Kintz, Carrie. "Joel Osteen Just Explained Why He Refuses to Speak On Hell." December 20, 2020. https://www.churchleaders.com/pastors/276763-joel-osteen-wont-preach-about-hell-but-he-should.html.

Knust, Jennifer W. *Unprotected Texts: The Bible's Surprising Contradictions about Sex and Desire*. New York: HarperCollins, 2011.

Konner, Joan. *The Atheist's Bible: An Illustrous Collection of Irreverent Thoughts*. New York: HarperCollins, 2007.

Kwon, Lillian. "Interview: Brian McLaren on Sin, Hell, New Kind of Christianity." *The Christian Post*, March 8, 2010. https://www.christianpost.com/news/interview-brian-mclaren-on-sin-hell-new-kind-of-christianity.html.

Laurino, Maria. "Unwanted Infant? Just Deposit Here." *The New Republic* (July-August 2023) 28–37.

Lee University. "Statement of Beliefs Concerning Human Sexuality and Gender: Appendix A: Student Handbook: 2024–2025." https://www.leeuniversity.edu/wp-content/upoloads/Student-Handbook.pdf.

Leigey, Margaret. "For the Longest Time: The Adjustment of Inmates to a Sentence of Life without Parole." *The Prison Journal* 90 (3) (2010) 247–68.

Lewis, Sinclair. *Babbitt*. New York: Harcourt, Brace, & World, 1961.

Lieber, David. "This Prosperity Preacher Makes No Bones about It: Cash Is King." *Dallas News*, April 26, 2019. https://www.dallasnews.com/news/watchdog/2019/04/26/this-prosperity-preacher-makes-no-bones-about-it-cash-is-king-and-he-says-he-has-a-lot-of-it.

Lutheran Church-Missouri Synod. "FAQs about LCMS Views: Death Penalty." https://www.lcms.org/about/beliefs/faqs/lcms-views#death-penalty.

——— "FAQs about LCMS Views: Family, Marriage and Human Sexuality." https://www.lcms.org/about/beliefs/faqs/lcms-views#family.

———. "FAQS about LCMS Views: Response to Homosexuality." August 20, 2020. https://www.lcms.org/about/beliefs/faqs/lcms-views#homosexuality.

Marietta, Don E. "On Using People." *Ethics* 82 (1972) 232–38.

Bibliography

Martin, Nina. "U.S. Bishops Take Aim at Sterilization." Propublica, December 30, 2014. https://www.propublica.org/article/u.s.-bishops-take-aim-at-sterilizaation.

Masters, Jarvis. *Finding Freedom: Writings from Death Row.* Junction City, CA: Padma, 1997.

Matheson, Alison. "PCUSAVotes to Allow Openly Gay Clergy." May 11, 2011. https://www.christianpost.com/news/presbyterian-church-usa-votes-to-allow-openly-gay-clergy.html.

Mayol-Garcia, Yeris, et al. *Number, Timing and Duration of Marriages and Divorces.* U. S. Census Bureau, April 22, 2021. https://www.census.gov/library/publications/2021/demo/p70-167.html.

MacFarquhar, Larissa. "The Fog: Adoptees Reckon with the Secrets of the Adoption Industry and Its Emotional Cost." *New Yorker* (April 10, 2023).

McCarthy, Justin. "Same-Sex Marriage Support Inches Up to New High of 71%." Gallup, June 1, 2022. https://news.gallup.com/poll/393197/same-sex-marriage-support-inches-new-high.aspx.

McGlasson, Paul C. *Choose You This Day: The Gospel of Jesus Christ and the Politics of Trumpism.* Eugene, OR: Cascade, 2019.

McLaren, Brian D. *A New Kind of Christianity: Ten Questions That Are Transforming the Faith.* New York: HarperOne, 2010.

Meaney, Joseph. "The Silent Plague of Vasectomies." National Catholic Bioethics Center, July 29, 2022. https://www.ncbcenter.org/messages-from-presidents/vasectomy.

Miller, Lisa. *Heaven: Our Enduring Fascination with the Afterlife.* New York: HarperCollins, 2010.

Mitchell, Stephen. *The Gospel According to Jesus: A New Translation and Guide to His Essential Teaching for Believers and Unbelievers.* New York: HarperCollins, 1991.

Moultrie, Monique. *Passionate and Pious: Religious Media and Black Women's Sexuality.* Durham: Duke University Press, 2017.

Nagin, Daniel S., and John V. Pepper, eds. *Deterrence and the Death Penalty.* Washington, DC: National Research Council: The National Academies, 2012.

National Association of Evangelicals. "Allowing Natural Death." 2014. https://www.nae.org/allowing-natural-death/.

National Catholic Register. "Cardinal Marx: 'The Catechism Is Not Set in Stone. One Is Also Allowed to Doubt What It Says.'" March 31, 2022. https://www.ncregister.com/cna/cardinal-marx-the-catechism-is-not-set-in-stone-one-is-also-allowed-to-doubt-what-it-says.

NBC News. "Presbyterian Church (USA) Recognizes Same-Sex Marriage." March 17, 2015. https://www.nbcnews.com/news/us-news/presbyterian-church-recognizes-same-sex-marriage-n325406.

Nellis, Ashley. *Life in Prison without Parole in* Louisiana. Washington, DC: The Sentencing Project, 2024.

———. *The Lives of Juvenile Lifers: Findings from a National Survey.* The Sentencing Project, March 2012. https://www.sentencingproject.org/reports/the-lives-of-juvenile-lifers-findings-from-a-national-survey/.

———. *No End in Sight: America's Enduring Reliance on Life Imprisonment.* Washington, DC: The Sentencing Project, 2021.

NewsChannel9. "Some Students Criticize Leaked Lee University's 'Statement of Belief' on LBGTQ issues." May 10, 2022. https://newschannel9.com/news/local/some-students-criticize-new-lee-university-statement-of-belief-on-lgbtq-issues.

Bibliography

New York Times. "Episcopal Canon on Divorce Eased." October 10, 1973. https://www.nytimes.com/1973/10/10/archives/episcopal-canon-on-divorce-eased-church-parley-liberalizes-rules.html.

Nortey, Justin, et al. "Few Americans Blame God or Say Faith Has Been Shaken Amid Pandemic, Other Tragedies." Pew Research Center, November 23, 2021. https://www.pewresearch.org/religion/2021/11/23/few-americans-blame-god-or-say-faith-has-been-shaken-amid-pandemic-other-tragedies/.

Osteen, Joel. *Become a Better You: 7 Keys to Improving Your Life Every Day.* New York: Free Press, 2007.

———. *Blessed in the Darkness: How All Things Are Working for Your Good.* New York: Hachette, 2017.

———. *Empty Out the Negative: Make Room for More Joy, Greater Confidence, and New Levels of Influence.* New York: Faith Words, 2020.

———. *Rule Your Day: 6 Keys to Maximizing Your Success and Accelerating Your Dreams.* Nashville & New York: Faith Words, 2022.

———. *Think Better: Live Better.* New York: Faith Words, 2016.

———. *Your Greater Is Coming: Discover the Path to Your Bigger, Better, and Brighter Future.* Nashville & New York: Faith Words, 2022.

Pacholczyk, Tad. "The 'Quality of Life' Error." *The East Tennessee Catholic,* August 6, 2023, A3.

Parker, Kim, and Rachel Minkin. "Public Has Mixed Views on the American Family." Pew Research Center, September 14, 2023. https://www.pewresearch.org/social-trends/2023/09/14/public-has-mixed-views-on-the-modern-american-family/.

Peale, Norman V. *The Power of Positive Thinking.* New York: Touchstone, 2015.

Pentin, Edward. "The Synod: A New Springtime or Pandora's Box?" *The East Tennessee Catholic,* December 3, 2023, A3.

Persaud, Winston D., and Ann L. Fritschel. "Pondering Eternity, Heaven and Hell." *Living Lutheran,* March 27, 2017. https://www.livinglutheran.org/2017/03/pondering-eternity-heaven-hell.

Peters, Rebecca T. *Trust Women: A Progressive Christian Argument for Reproductive Justice.* Boston: Beacon, 2018.

Pew Research Center. "America's Abortion Quandary." May 6, 2022. https://www.pewresearch.org/religion/2022/05/06/americans-abortion-quandary/.

———. "Attitudes on Same-Sex Marriage: Public Opinion on Same-Sex Marriage." May 14, 2019. https://www.pewresearch.org/religion/fact-sheet/changing-attitudes-on-gay-marriage/.

———. "Modeling the Future of Religion in America." September 13, 2022. https://www.pewresearch.org/religion/2022/09/13/modeling-the-future-of-religion-in-america/.

Pope Francis. *Encyclical Fratelli Tutti (All Brothers).* October 3, 2020. https://www.vatican.va/content/francesco/en/encyclicals/documents/papa-francesco-20201003-enciclica-fratelli-tutti.html.

Prejean, Helen. *Dead Man Walking: An Eyewitness Account of the Death Penalty in the United States.* New York: Vintage, 1994.

Presbyterian Church (USA). "Abortion/Reproductive Choice Issues." February 23, 2016. https://centernet.pcusa.org/blog/abortion-issues-2/.

———. "What We Believe: Capital Punishment." https://centernet.pcusa.org/what-we-believe/capital punishment/.

Bibliography

———. "What We Believe: Sexuality and Same-Gender Relationships." https://centernet.pcusa.org/what-we-believe/sexuality-and-same-gender-relationships/.

Prothero, Stephen. "The Bible's Contradictions about Sex: BU Theologian: The Good Book Is Not a Rule Book." February 6, 2011. https://www.bu.edu/articles/2011/the-bibles-contradictions-about-sex/.

Rasmussen, Joshua. *How Reason Can Lead to God: A Philosopher's Bridge to Faith*. Downers Grove, IL: InterVarsity, 2019.

Ray, Rashawn, and Hoda Mahmoudi, eds. *Systematic Racism in America: Sociological Theory, Education Inequality, and Social Change*. New York: Routledge, 2022.

Reagan, Leslie J. *When Abortion Was a Crime: Women, Medicine, and Law in the United States, 1867–1973*. Berkeley, CA: University of California Press, 2022.

Relevant Magazine. "Report: 38% of Evangelical churchgoers believe in the 'Prosperity Gospel.'" August 6, 2018. https://www.relevant.com.

Roach, David. "SBC not 'Third Way.'" *Baptist Press*, October 23, 2014. www.https://baptistcourier.com/2014/10/sbc-third-way-divorce/.

Saad, Lydia. "Americans' Abortion Views Steady in Past Year." Gallup Poll, June 29, 2020. https://news.gallup.com/poll/313094/americans-abortion-views-steady-past-year/aspx.

———. "Broader Support for Abortion Continues Post-Dobbs." Gallup Poll, June 14, 2023. https://news.gallup.com/poll/506759/broader-support-abortion-rights-continues-post-dobbs.aspx.

Salai, Sean. "Barna Study Suggests 'Christians in Name Only' Skew Polls of U.S. Believers." *National Catholic Register*, March 21, 2022. https://www.ncregister.com/news/barna-study-suggests-christians-in-name-only-skew-political-polls-of-us-believers.

Scalia, Antonin. "God's Justice and Ours." *First Things: A Monthly Journal of Religion and Public Life* 5 (2002) 17–21.

Seidel, Andrew L. *The Founding Myth: Why Christian Nationalism Is Un-American*. New York: Sterling, 2019.

Shelly, Rubel. *Divorce and Remarriage: A Redemptive Theology*. Abilene, TX: Leafwood, 2007.

Sherwood, Harriet. "Pope Francis Backs Same-Sex Civil Unions." *The Guardian*, October 21, 2020. https://www.theguardian.com/world/oct/21/pope-francis-backs-same-sex-civil-unions.

Silliman, Daniel. *Reading Evangelicals: How Christian Fiction Shaped a Culture and a Faith*. Grand Rapids, MI: Eerdmans, 2021.

Sinitiere, Phillip L. *Salvation with a Smile: Joel Osteen, Lakewood Church, and American Christianity*. New York: New York University Press.

Smith, Gregory A., et al. "Religious 'Nones' in America: Who They Are and What They Believe." Pew Research Center January 24, 2024. https://www.pewresearch.org/religion/2024/01/24/religious-nones-in-america-who-they-are-and-what-they-believe/.

Smith, Peter. "Southern Baptists Considering Which Republican to Support." *Johnson City Press*, June 8, 2023, A7.

Souryal, Sam S., and John Whitehead. *Ethics in Criminal Justice: In Search of the Truth*. New York, Routledge, 2020.

Southern Baptist Convention. "On Celebrating the Advancement of Pro-Life Legislation in State Legislatures." June 1, 2019. https://www.sbc.net/resource-library/resolutions/on-celebrating-the-advancement-of-pro-life-legilsation-in-state-legislatures/.

———. "On the Reality of Hell." June 1, 2011. https://www.sbc.net/resource-library/resolutions/on-the-reality-of-hell/.

———. "On the Sanctity of Human Life." June 1, 2015. https://www.sbc.net/resource-library/resolutions/on-the-sanctity-of-human-life/.

———. "On the Sufficiency of Scripture Regarding the Afterlife." June 1, 2014. https://www.sbc.net/resource-library/resolutions/on-the-sufficiency-of-scripture-regarding-the-afterlife/.

———. "Resolution on Euthanasia and Assisted Suicide." June 1, 1992. https://www/sbc.net/resource-library/resolutions/resolution-on-euthanasia-and-assisted-suicide/.

———. "Resolution on Homosexuality." June 16, 1988. https://www.sbc.net/resource-library/resolutions/resolution-on-homosexuality-5/.

———. "Resolution on Human Sexuality." June 1, 1991. https://www.sbc.net/resource-library/resolution-on-human-sexuality/.

Spodaro, Antonio. "The Water Has Been Agitated: Francis in Conversation with Jesuits in Portugal." *La Civilta Cattolica*, August 28, 2023. https://www.laciviltacattolica.com/the water-has-been-agitated/.

Stimson, Andrew, and Charles Grossman. *Adult Time for Adult Crime: Life Without Parole for Juvenile Killers and Violent Teens*. The Heritage Foundation August 2009. https://www.heritage.org/crime-and-justice/report/adult-time-adult-crimes-life-without-parole-juvenile-killers-and-violent-teens.

Stulberg, Debra B., et al. "Tubal Ligation in Catholic Hospitals: A Qualitative Study of Ob-Gyns' Experiences." *Contraception* 90 (2014) 422–28.

Sullivan, Becky. "Pope Francis Approves Catholic Blessings for Same-Sex Couples, But Not for Marriage." *NPR*, December 18, 2023. https://www.npr.org/2023/12/18/1220077102/pope-francis-blessings-same-sex-couples.

Twain, Mark. *The Complete Short Stories*. New York: Everyman's Library, 2012.

United Church of Christ. "Equal Marriage Rights for All." Resolution adopted at the Twenty-Fifth General Synod July 4, 2005. https://new.uccfiles.com/pdf/2005-EQUAL-MARRIAGE-RIGHTS-FOR-ALL.pdf.

United Lutheran Church in America (ULCA). "Marriage, Family, and Divorce." https://www.resources.elca.org.

United Methodist Church. "United Methodist Social Principles: The Social Community." https://www.umcjustice.org/en/content/social-principles-the-social-community.

United States Conference of Catholic Bishops. *Catechism of the Catholic Church* 2nd ed., 2016. https://www.usccb.c/d.bz/Catchism-of-the-Catholic-Church/.

———. *Ethical and Religious Directives for Catholic Health Care Services*, 2018. https://www.usccb.org/resources/ethical-and-religious-directives-catholic-healthcare-services.

———. "Statement on Capital Punishment." (1980). https://www.usccb.org/resources/bishops-statement-capital-punishment-1980.

———. *A Synodal Church in Mission: Synthesis Report*. October 28, 2023. https://www.synod.va/content/dam/synod.assembly/synthesis/english/2023.10.28-ENG-Synthesis-Report.

Vasoli, Robert H. (1998). *What God Has Joined Together: The Annulment Crisis in American Catholicism*. New York: Oxford University Press.

Vines, Matthew. *God and the Gay Christian: The Biblical Case in Support of Same-Sex Relationships*. New York: Convergent, 2014.

Bibliography

Wade, Lisa. *American Hookup: The New Culture of Sex on Campus.* New York: Norton, 2017.

Weems, Renita. *What Matters Most: Ten Lessons in Living Passionately from the Song of Solomon.* New York: Walk Worthy, 2004.

Whitehead, Andrew L. *American Idolatry: How Christian Nationalism Betrays the Gospel and Threatens the Church.* Grand Rapids, MI: Brazos, 2023.

Whitehead, Andrew L., and Samuel L Perry. *Taking America Back for God: Christian Nationalism in the United States.* New York: Oxford University Press, 2020.

Wiering, Maria. "Bishop Barron Criticizes Part of Synod Report." *The East Tennessee Catholic*, December 3, 2023, A3.

Winfield, Nicole. "Activists Hope Pope's Approval of Same-Sex Blessings Could Ease Anti-LGBTQ+ Bias and Repression." *AP News,* December 19, 2023. https://www.apnews.com/articles/vatican-lgbtq-pope-blessings-29b1c90f245170f7cfa81a0d1dadac0.

Wright, N. T. *Hope, Not Fear: Changing the Way We View Death.* Lanham, MD: Rowman & Littlefield, 2018.

———. *Simply Jesus: A New Vision of Who He Was, What He Did, and Why He Matters.* New York: HarperOne, 2011.

Young, David. *A Grand Illusion: How Progressive Christianity Undermines Biblical Faith.* 2019. https://www.Renew.org/product/grand-illusion/.

Zimmerman, Paul R. "Estimates of the Deterrent Effect of Alternative Execution Methods in the United States: 1978–2000." *American Journal of Economics & Sociology* 65 (2006) 909–41.

www.ingramcontent.com/pod-product-compliance
Lightning Source LLC
Chambersburg PA
CBHW072135160426
43197CB00012B/2113